The Church is Dead

REFLECTIONS OF A GAY CHRISTIAN

Paul C Svensen

Melbourne, Australia

Copyright © 2022 by Paul C Svensen.

All rights reserved. No part of this publication may be reproduced, distributed or transmitted in any form or by any means, including photocopying, recording, or other electronic or mechanical methods, without the prior written permission of the publisher, except in the case of brief quotations embodied in critical reviews and certain other noncommercial uses permitted by copyright law. For permission requests, write to the publisher, addressed "Attention: Permissions Coordinator," at the address below.

Paul C Svensen C/- Intertype Publish and Print
Unit 45, 125 Highbury Road
BURWOOD VIC 3125
www.intertype.com.au

Ordering Information:
Quantity sales. Special discounts are available on quantity purchases by corporations, associations, and others. For details, contact the "Special Sales Department" at the address above.

The Church is Dead/ Paul C Svensen. —1st ed.
ISBN 978-0-6455238-3-6

Contents

Acknowledgements 5

Foreword 7

Prologue 11

God 17

    Who Is God? 17

    The Ten Commandments 25

    Grace 28

    God and Gays 28

    Only One Way 31

    What Does God Intend for Us? 33

    Qarah 37

Man 41

    We Are All Sinners 41

    What Has Happened in the Last 2,000 Years? 41

    Whose Are You? 46

The Church 49

    Pre-Reformation Times 51

- The Industrial Revolution 52
- What Drives Us – and the Church? 52
- False Prophets 54
- The Forest and the Trees 57
- Misinterpretation of the Bible 58
- Of Wine and Wineskins 67
- What about Other Religions? 70
- Christian Churches 79
- Why the Church Is Wrong 85
- Why People Don't Attend Church 94
- What the Church Must Do 95

The Bible 101
- What Does the Bible REALLY Say? 101

What Do You Need to Do Now? 109
- Acknowledge that Jesus Has Paid the Penalty for Your Sins . 110
- Love God and Others 111
- Simply Trust Him 112
- He Wants, and Demands, All of You 113

    Express Gratitude 116

    Freedom within Boundaries.................................. 116

    What Does God Expect of You?........................... 117

    On Pottery.. 118

    Prayer of Response 119

A Glorious Future 121

    Life Here and Now 121

    Death.. 124

    End Times 125

    Heaven 126

    Hell.. 128

Appendix.. 131

    Extracts from the Roman Catholic Catechism 131

Acknowledgements

My sister, Randi Svensen, spent many hours editing the draft manuscript of **The Church Is Dead**. Author of a number of historical books, including **Wooden Boats, Iron Men – The Halvorsen Story**, Randi's critical eye was invaluable as this first-time author tried to negotiate the murky waters of literary enterprise. I couldn't believe how many errors I had made! Randi also had many constructive suggestions for making the content more readable. I am extremely grateful to her for all the effort she put into this endeavour.

Chan, my husband, has been the love of my life for 17 years. I'm very grateful for Chan's patience (a bit of which I hope has rubbed off onto me) and for his support, especially in some of the tough times we've faced.

My daughters, Ruth and Heather, have continued to love and support me, even after I turned their lives upside down when I abandoned them upon finally accepting the fact that I was gay.

My good friend, Stephen Waterhouse, made a great many suggestions for changes to the manuscript, as well as picking up a number of errors I had made. I am extremely grateful to Stephen for his thoroughness and his gentleness – even in rebuke!

Finally, and most importantly, I want to thank my Lord, Jesus Christ, without whose guidance throughout the whole writing of this book it would not have been written. What an amazing God we serve! He actually encouraged me to attack the institution that we call the Church, reminding me of when, in a fit of rage, He overturned the tables of the money changers and traders outside the temple in Jerusalem. Jesus is the One who will get the praise for this book, though hopefully not the condemnation!

Foreword

As a gay Christian, I have often been ostracised by the Church. However, knowing that God Himself is not homophobic, I set out to investigate church beliefs. This led to some interesting discoveries, prompting me to write this book.

When I set out to write **The Church Is Dead**, my main intention was to expose the hypocrisy of the Christian Church in its handling of the hot topic of homosexuality. But it soon became evident that there was something much bigger at play here. I discovered that churches of all denominations have watered down the Gospel message, completely missing the point of James' statement that *"faith without deeds is dead"* (James 2:26). The Gospel is not opposed to *effort*, but to *earning*.

This actually isn't anything new. Paul expressed his own frustration 2,000 years ago with the believers in Galatia:

"You foolish Galatians! Who has bewitched you? Before your very eyes Jesus Christ was clearly portrayed as crucified. I would like to learn just one thing from you: Did you receive the Spirit by the works of the law, or by believing what you heard? Are you so foolish? After beginning by means of the Spirit, are you now trying to finish by means of the flesh?" (Galatians 3:1-3).

In her excellent book, **The Suicidal Church**[1], Caroline Miley says something with which I agree wholeheartedly:

> Over the two millennia since its origins, a huge, lumbering, hierarchical and bureaucratic institution has been erected over the empty sepulchre of its simple and charismatic Founder and His message. <u>One of the church's most striking failings has been the way in which this edifice, by its very existence</u>

---

[1] © Caroline Miley, 2002

<u>and nature, has obscured, even contradicted, the message of new life offered by its Leader</u> [my emphasis].

The Roman Catholic Church in particular seems to have learned little in the five centuries since Martin Luther nailed his **95 Theses** to the door of his church in Wittenberg, Germany. They were basically 95 issues where Luther believed Catholic doctrine was at odds with the Bible. He sent a copy to the Archbishop of Mainz in October 1517, hoping to initiate a discussion within the church leadership on his radical views. But the Archbishop was not even prepared to engage Luther in a dialogue on the issues he had raised. When Luther refused to recant his statements, Pope Leo X in 1521 excommunicated him and he was condemned as an outlaw by the Holy Roman Emperor. Luther promulgated the fact that salvation is by grace alone, not by works, thereby giving birth to the Protestant church. He condemned the practice of selling *indulgences*, whereby a layman could buy a certificate from his priest to reduce the punishment for his sins that he would have to undergo after death. During Luther's time, the Pope got his chief indulgences commissioner to urge parish priests to sell as many indulgences as possible, as the money so earned would help fund the building of St Peter's Basilica. Sadly, even other churches today engage in the selling of indulgences, although they don't put it quite so bluntly. I will speak, for example, of the American preacher Joyce Meyer's instructions to her own congregation on the subject of tithing. Luther also challenged the Catholic Church's teaching on *sacerdotalism* – that is, that priests were the intermediaries between God and man. Moreover, Luther translated the Bible from Latin into the German vernacular, which upset the Catholic hierarchy as it meant that lay people could finally read it for themselves. Unbelievably, even when I was a boy some Roman Catholic Churches still conducted their services in Latin, making it impossible – no doubt, deliberately – for church attendees to even understand what was being preached. Priests believed that laymen did not, in any case, have the ability to interpret the Bible. In retrospect, the opposite was probably true!

Luther also challenged another important tenet of the Roman Catholic Church at that time – the concept of papal infallibility – having observed that the Pope did occasionally make mistakes, just as we all do. I suspect that most

Roman Catholics still believe the Pope is infallible. If he says that black is blue, who are they to argue?

I wrote **The Church Is Dead** 500 years after Luther's excommunication by the Roman Catholic Church. Like Luther, I will probably suffer widespread condemnation for my attacks on the established Church, but I don't believe it can be allowed to continue misleading the world regarding the most critical issue that has ever existed: Salvation. It is my fervent prayer that church leaders right across the world will sit up and take notice, thereby reviving Luther's entreaties regarding the truth about salvation.

There are more than 1.3 billion Roman Catholics in the world, most of whom continue to be misled by their church leaders on the subject of salvation. Sadly, though, it's not only the Catholics who have been so grievously misled. Most Protestant churches would not admit to including works in their formula for salvation, but the debate within the Protestant Church regarding homosexuality has revealed the general belief that faith in Jesus is not sufficient for salvation; that if we continue to sin, God will condemn us to Hell, negating the final statement that Jesus made on the cross: *"It is finished"* (John 19:30).

I make much in this book about what matters to God. He doesn't care *who* you are or *what* you are. All that matters to Him is *whose* you are. You belong to God or to Satan. There is no other option for you. The moment you die you will find yourself in the home of one or the other of them: In Heaven, or in Hell. If you don't yet belong to God, it is the responsibility of the Christians you come across to introduce you to Him.

God has given each one of us free will. You have the absolute freedom to choose where you will spend eternity. A famous theologian, CS Lewis, described Hell as *"the greatest monument to human freedom"*. He then added, *"There are only two kinds of people: Those who say to God, 'Thy will be done', and those to whom God says, in the end, 'Thy will be done'"*. One day you will pass from this life to the next one. It will be too late then for you to change your mind about following God.

I hope you are reading this book because you seek the truth. As the Christian writer John North said of the desire for truth in his **Time with God** devotional of 16 September 2019: *"Not well-argued, well-preached, well-*

structured, but lifeless truth. No, [people] seek truth that has been experienced, truth that has been lived out, truth that has stood the test of time and has not withered in the storms of life". I am not theologically trained. I don't pastor a church. I am not in some other form of full-time ministry. But I have a story to share. It is a story moulded through 45 years of sitting at the feet of my Lord and Saviour, Jesus Christ.

That's not to minimise the wonderful teaching I have received over those decades from some truly gifted pastors, as well as guidance and direction from Christian family and friends. While I have been greatly blessed by those people, the direct involvement of my Lord Jesus Christ in my life is what is moulding me into the man He wants me to be. I believe that is something He wants for all of us.

Prologue

But there were also false prophets among the people, just as there will be false teachers among you. They will secretly introduce destructive heresies, even denying the sovereign Lord who bought them – bringing swift destruction on themselves.
2 Peter 2:1

Two thousand years after Jesus died the most lonely and painful death imaginable, in order to provide a way for His people to gain eternal life, the Christian Church is still unable to explain and proclaim faithfully its message of salvation to the whole world.

Why do you think that is? Is it because so many governments now ban praying and the teaching of Scripture in schools? Is it because the media commonly seize on any opportunity to embarrass the Church or its leaders? Is it because there are so many other things competing with the Church for our attention? Is it because so many high-profile church leaders are perceived as hypocrites? No, it is none of those things. The problem can be laid fairly and squarely at the feet of the Church itself. This book attempts to expose the fundamental flaw of the Church today.

Have you come across the term *anamorphosis*? It dates back to the 16th century, when the Italian artist, Tommaso Laureti, intentionally distorted a work of art so that it could only be recognised from a particular angle. For example, a sculpture might consist of a series of apparently-random vertical poles which, when viewed from a particular angle – and that angle only – reveals the face of a famous person.

In a similar way, the Bible needs to be looked at from a particular perspective if it is to be read as God intended. Sadly, I believe that the Church in general presents as unable to interpret the Bible correctly, as it is looking at it from the wrong perspective.

This is why Christians have misused the Bible for the last 2,000 years. It's why Christians believed that God condoned slavery until 1833 in England and 1865 in America. It's why interracial marriage was banned in the US until 1967. It's why coloured people are often still not encouraged to mix with whites – even in church. It's why women are still treated as inferior to men in some denominations.

The Church is dead! I have written this book as a wake-up call to the Church, which has misunderstood the significance of the New Testament. The word *testament* comes from the Greek word for *covenant*, and it is effectively a will. A will can only come into effect with the death of the one leaving it, so the New Covenant only came into effect when Jesus died on the cross. His last words, *"It is finished"*, confirmed that Jesus had accomplished what He had set out to do: To replace the old covenant of *Law* with the new one of *Grace*.

The Old Testament prophet Ezekiel, who lived 2,600 years ago, must have wondered if his people were ever going to understand what God was saying to them. I wonder the same thing today. In Chapter 37 of Ezekiel's book, the Lord asked this question when He set Ezekiel in the Valley of Dry Bones: *"Son of man, can these bones live?"* Sadly, today's churches for the most part are full of dead bodies. Incidentally, the following chapter of Ezekiel is full of prophecies about the *End Times*, most of which have already come to pass.

I make no apology for my all-out attack on the established Church. It is not just the Church's vilification of gays that upsets me: It has been sending the wrong message to *everyone* about salvation, somehow maintaining that God requires us to follow all the Old Testament commandments if we are to retain our salvation, or even to be blessed by God in this life. Some churches today do have this right, but unfortunately they are far too few and often their congregations still hold to the errors.

I have tried to downplay in this book my anger with the Church, though I may come across to some of my readers as bitter. Now I am actually more sad than angry: Sad that the Church in general is failing God. This has resulted in a determination to put the record straight regarding Christianity.

A good friend of mine told me that he wondered why so many Christians over fifty years old dropped out of church, and how difficult it was for them (including himself) to be 'refreshed in the Lord'. Pondering on his observation a bit later, I thought of two possible reasons for this. Firstly, that the Church has lost its *congruence*. In other words, it no longer practises what it preaches. It has become too worldly, and it preaches salvation by works, as well as by faith. The second reason is that I believe some older people have become disillusioned with life in general, and with God in particular. They have lost their focus on Jesus. They look back on all their dreams and aspirations, and realise that things didn't work out as they had planned. So they blame God, and decide it is no longer worth spending time with Him in church.

But I feel completely the opposite. Sure, my life did not turn out at all like I had planned. Disaster after disaster could have turned me away from God, but somehow they brought me closer to Him. Even now, as I look back on all the wrong choices I have made, and at all the disasters that have befallen me, I am filled with gratitude at how things turned out. The well-known song, **I'd Rather Have Jesus**[2], is very true for me. I don't have all the *silver* or *gold* that I had expected to have in my retirement, but I have enough. Moreover, I have Jesus, and that trumps anything the world could offer.

I believe that society has lost its way. The goals we aspire to are, generally speaking, diametrically opposed to the plans that God has for us. We have lost our connection to Jesus, living only for ourselves. But it's not just society in general that has lost its way. I believe that the Christian Church has failed to understand that the Old Covenant law of the Old Testament has given way *absolutely* to the New Covenant of grace. We seem to think that we need to add our own works to what Jesus has already achieved on the Cross for us. I believe this is the underlying reason why the Church rejects gay people, and it is something I will address in detail in this book.

You will learn that I am very critical of the Church in general. I need to point out, however, that there are many individual churches where the Gospel is proclaimed faithfully, and whose congregations truly love the Lord. But the point remains: Church attendance numbers, certainly in Australia, are in

---

[2] Rhea F Miller (1922)

an unprecedented decline. In the forty years to 2019, the proportion of Australians attending church at least once a month had dropped by more than half, from 36 per cent to 15 per cent. In the five years to 2016, the Anglican Church in Australia lost 580,000 of its 3.7 million members[3]. I believe these statistics reflect the fact that the message given by most churches is confusing to non-believers. Most of them – but not all – declare the Lordship of Jesus Christ, but they simply do not understand the role of the Old Testament since the New Covenant was ushered in with the death and resurrection of Jesus. The Roman Catholic Church, in particular, has trashed Jesus' message that salvation is only through Him.

The young pastor at a local Pentecostal church I attended for about five years remonstrated with me after he had read the draft of a booklet I had written, titled **Let Us Cross to the Other Side**. He asked me how I could dare to attack the Church, when it is Christ's *Bride*. This man failed to understand the difference between Jesus' meaning of *church*, and the institution that we broadly call *The Church*. The *Bride of Christ* is only mentioned once in the Bible, in Ephesians 5:22-24, though there are numerous instances in the Gospels where Jesus is described as the *Bridegroom*, therefore implying that there must have been a bride. Jesus' reference to *church* here is the body of believers, not the various institutions known as *The Church*. Paul's statement in his letter to the Ephesians – which, incidentally, has caused a lot of grief for wives! – says:

"Wives, submit to your own husbands as you do to the Lord. For the husband is the head of the wife as Christ is the head of the church, His body, of which He is the Saviour. Now as the church submits to Christ, so also wives should submit to their husbands in everything" (Ephesians 5:22-24).

Note that Paul said *"of which He is the Saviour"*. That should give a pretty good clue as to what he meant about the church: It was the body of believers. It's not the individual believers that I am condemning, but the church as an institution. And I want to stress again that there are a lot of individual churches operating under the mantle of a church denomination where the Gospel message is faithfully proclaimed.

---

[3] According to the 2016 Australian Census (Australian Bureau of Statistics)

In any discussion about salvation, it is important to remember the tension between *grace* and *truth*. Many churches tend to focus on one of those aspects, to the general exclusion of the other. Most of us enjoy listening to one of the most famous songs of all time, **Amazing Grace**. And grace *is* amazing. Paul said *"But God demonstrates His own love for us in this: While we were still sinners, Christ died for us"* (Romans 5:8). <u>While we were still sinners</u>!

I will explain in this book that we must not neglect the significance of truth. Jesus paid a terrible price for our salvation, but it is not automatic. Unless we acknowledge His sacrifice and ask His forgiveness, we will not be saved.

Grace is free for the asking, but it is not cheap. Both grace and truth need to be preached from the pulpit, and this book exposes the black hole that so many churches have fallen into by excluding either one or the other.

CHAPTER 1

God

This is love: Not that we loved God, but that He loved us.
1 John 4:10

Who Is God?

I think it is appropriate to begin this book with an explanation of who God actually is. After all, if we don't have any understanding of Him, how can we get to know Him?

Is God a hard, legalistic judge, out to catch anyone who sins? Or is He a *soft touch*, who wouldn't hurt a fly? People often accuse our Lord of being harsh, allowing innocent people to suffer from catastrophes that He has caused or at least allowed to happen, such as earthquakes and hurricanes. Others maintain that a God of love would never allow people to suffer, and so they don't believe that He even exists. What is He really like?

I admit that I don't know why God allows tsunamis to strike poor regions in Asia, wild storms to kill thousands of people in a matter of hours, or earthquakes to swallow up whole villages. But for me it is enough to know that God is good. The fact that He allowed His own precious Son to suffer a cruel death, that we deserve, is sufficient evidence that He doesn't experience some sort of malicious delight at the suffering of His people. *"What, then, shall we say in response to these things? If God is for us, who can be against us? He who did not spare His own Son, but gave Him up for us all – how will He not also, along with Him, graciously give us all things?"* (Romans 8:31-32)

You may have heard the story of the Just Judge. This man's son had found himself in the dock after he had committed an offence, his own father hearing the evidence against him. The judge probably would have liked to have pronounced his son not guilty, but the evidence against him was too strong, and the judge was a man of integrity. So the judge brought down his gavel and announced a guilty verdict, the penalty being the maximum fine for such an offence. But then he did a remarkable thing. He removed his judicial robes and wig, and went down to the cashier to pay his son's fine.

This story is a parable of our heavenly Father's relationship with us. We were guilty and, as a just Judge, God could not pretend that we were not. But He loves us so much that He paid the penalty Himself for our sins. God ceased to be my Judge when I invited Him into my life, becoming simply my loving Father. I still can't understand, after more than four decades as a Christian, how God could love me so much that He would make such a sacrifice for me!

A relative of mine told me in 2017 that a close friend of hers was dying of cancer and that she could not believe in a God who would allow someone to suffer as much as her friend was suffering at that time. I didn't have an explanation for her then, and I don't have one now. However, when I think of what it must have taken for God to turn His back on His own dear Son at the time Jesus needed Him most – and, make no mistake, that is exactly what He did – I can't possibly doubt His perfect love for all mankind. How it must have hurt God the Father when Jesus called out to Him from the cross: *"My God, my God, why have You forsaken Me?"* (Matthew 27:46). At that moment, Jesus knew total separation from His Father. Abraham Lincoln expressed his own feelings on this topic when he said, *"Sir, my concern is not whether God is on our side; my greatest concern is to be on God's side, for God is always right"*.

I have often been told by non-Christian friends that they are happy for me that I have such a belief in God: *Whatever works for you* is a common statement. But God will not be what people want Him to be. John North wrote in an issue of his daily devotional, **Time with God**:

> God does not, will not, cannot change. He is what He is. It doesn't matter what some people imagine God to be like, or what religions they follow. God

will not be who people want Him to be. He will not and cannot be anything other than what He is. He has revealed Himself in the Bible and in the person of Jesus Christ. Our job is not to decide what God is like, but to discover the God who is who He is! [my emphasis].

This is a very important concept to understand. It's not simply a matter of *whatever works for you*.

As a new Christian in 1977, I was excited to learn three attributes of God that answered so many questions I had had about Him:

- He is *omniscient*. There is absolutely nothing that He doesn't know.
- He is *omnipresent*. He is everywhere at once. Corrie ten Boom wrote in her most famous book, **The Hiding Place**[4], that she had discovered *"there is no pit so deep that God's love is not deeper still"*. He will never leave us nor forsake us.
- He is *omnipotent*. There is nothing that He cannot do, except go against His own character. I have discovered that for myself in miracle after miracle. This is where I feel sad that Albert Einstein missed out. While he acknowledged that there had to be a Supreme Creator of the Universe, this otherwise brilliant man could not believe that God would ever suspend what he considered to be His 'immutable laws'. Incidentally, Einstein has been credited with this famous observation (although it appears to have been coined many years before by Edwin Conklin, who was President of the American Association for the Advancement of Science, in 1936): *"The probability of life originating from accident is comparable to the probability of the Unabridged Dictionary resulting from an explosion in a print shop"*.

Here are some of the things that Einstein said about God:

- *"Every scientist becomes convinced that the laws of nature manifest the existence of a spirit vastly superior to that of men"*.
- *"Everyone who is seriously involved in the pursuit of science becomes convinced that a spirit is manifest in the laws of the universe – a spirit vastly superior to that of man"*.

---

[4] © 1971 and 1984, Corrie ten Boom and Elizabeth and John Sherrill

- *"The divine reveals itself in the physical world".*
- *"My God created laws ... His universe is not ruled by wishful thinking but by immutable laws".*
- *"I want to know how God created this world. I want to know His thoughts".*
- *"What I am really interested in knowing is whether God could have created the world in a different way".*

Most people believe that the only way to reach Heaven is to climb the ladder of goodness to it. Some even have their ladder up against the wrong wall. Even if they attempt to climb the ladder that Jacob saw – the one that actually does lead to Heaven – they will never make it to the top. Genesis 28:12-13 recounts what happened to Jacob while he was sleeping on his way to Harran: *"He had a dream in which he saw a stairway resting on the Earth, with its top reaching to Heaven, and the angels of God were ascending and descending on it. There above it stood the Lord, and He said: 'I am the Lord, the God of your father Abraham and the God of Isaac'"*. The problem we have is that we have to be perfect to be admitted into Heaven, and no one, other than Jesus Himself, has ever lived a perfect life on this Earth. Knowing that we could never make it there on our own, Jesus came down that stairway to us, and paid the penalty that was ours, as punishment for our sins.

The Trinity

Jesus Christ claimed to be God, saying, *"I and the Father are one"* (John 10:30). It is not my job here to convince you of the truth of Jesus' deity via circumstantial evidence, such as the Bible and the writings of historians from Jesus' time on Earth. However, if you are into statistics, take note of this: The late Professor Peter W Stoner said in his book, **Science Speaks**[5], that there are 60 major messianic prophecies[6] in the Old Testament that were fulfilled when Jesus came to Earth. The odds of only eight of those having come true in one

---

[5] © 2002, Moody Press Chicago

[6] Some Old Testament scholars claim there are actually 351 such prophecies, but not all of them are considered "major".

man are 1:100,000 trillion. And it is important to remember that the prophecies were all written many hundreds of years before Jesus' birth.

CS Lewis, author of many excellent theological books, as well as such children's classics as **The Lion, the Witch and the Wardrobe**, made a comment in **Mere Christianity** that has been quoted in countless publications over the years:

> I am trying here to prevent anyone saying the really foolish thing that people often say about Him: I'm ready to accept Jesus as a great moral teacher, but I don't accept his claim to be God. That is the one thing we must not say. A man who was merely a man and said the sort of things Jesus said would not be a great moral teacher. He would either be a lunatic – on the level with the man who says he is a poached egg – or else he would be the Devil of Hell. You must make your choice. Either this man was, and is, the Son of God, or else a madman or something worse. You can shut him up for a fool, you can spit at him and kill him as a demon or you can fall at his feet and call him Lord and God, but let us not come with any patronizing nonsense about his being a great human teacher. He has not left that open to us. He did not intend to. ... Now it seems to me obvious that He was neither a lunatic nor a fiend: and consequently, however strange or terrifying or unlikely it may seem, I have to accept the view that He was and is God.

The Holy Spirit had visited a number of Old Testament characters for specific purposes, and in most cases only at specific times. When He appeared to His followers after His resurrection, Jesus promised to send the Holy Spirit to them. The Holy Spirit is the third Person in the Trinity: Father, Son and Holy Spirit. He lives permanently in New Testament believers.

It is difficult for people with finite minds to comprehend the concept of a *Triune God*. How can He be three people in one? God actually enjoys fellowship with Himself! I believe that is why He endowed us with the ability to enter into relationships with each other, as well as with Him.

His Holiness

So what is the Bible really about? Almost all of the 66 books, from Genesis to Revelation, talk of God's redemptive plan for mankind through Jesus. Its entire content is about love, grace, forgiveness and, yes, holiness. God's holiness is imparted to His followers.

Does the church believe that straight Christians are holy, but gay ones aren't? In God's eyes, I am holy, and I am perfect. How can that be? It's because His Son, Jesus, bore all my sins – past, present and future – as He also bears yours, if you will only ask Him to come into your life.

But what is holiness? The original Greek word is *hagiasmos*, which means sanctification; that is, a holy person is one who has been set apart for God. God said: *"For I will forgive their wickedness and will remember their sins no more"* (Hebrews 8:12).

I didn't become holy because of my good works. I became holy because of Jesus' sacrifice on the cross.

The Bible tells us that *"whatever does not proceed from faith is sin"* (Romans 14:23), and it is true that most sin finds its root in a failure to trust God. When Satan tempted Eve, she chose to trust Satan's words and her own judgement more than God.

Almost any sin in your life can be expressed in the words, "God, I cannot get what I need to fulfil me in life from You. I need to get it from this other thing". Satan caused Eve to be dissatisfied with God's way of life, and to think she needed more in order to be fulfilled. What a deception!

Pursuing fulfilment outside God's will for us is like drinking salt water to quench our thirst: It feels good going down, but we end up thirstier than before.

God designed us in such a way that we will only find what we need in Him.

I used to focus my witnessing to others on the strength of God's holiness, rather than concentrating on His amazing love. I would say that, since God is holy, He cannot allow unforgiven sin into His Heaven. That is true, of course, but I have learned that people don't want to know they have been condemned to Hell, even when I try to show them how to avoid that fate.

God showed us how much He loved us when He allowed His precious Son to pay the penalty for our sins: *"But God demonstrates His own love for us in this: While we were still sinners, Christ died for us"* (Romans 5:8).

Randy Kilgore wrote in **Our Daily Bread**, one of the devotionals I read daily, on 8 December 2017: "Most people know they're messed up. Instead of lectures, they need a hope for redemption. Stern faces or sharp words can *block their view of that hope. Like Ananias (see Acts 9:12), ... followers of Jesus must become the face of grace in these life-changing encounters with others".*

But God cannot simply forget our sins. Many people today are of the view that a loving, gracious God would not condemn anyone to Hell. But His character makes it impossible for Him to forgive sin without attaching a penalty to it. This is precisely the reason that He sent His own beloved Son, Jesus, to die on our behalf. When you accept Jesus as your Lord and Saviour, you can rest assured that your sins are forgiven – permanently. This forgiveness covers our past sins, those we may be committing at this very moment, and those we are yet to commit. I believe that God does not even see my sins any more. Christians don't need to keep asking God for forgiveness. He has already forgiven us.

Does that mean that we can freely sin? No! But not because it will change God's position. I believe it is purely for our own sake. You have probably heard the saying, "If God suddenly seems far away, guess who moved!". And that is absolutely true. God hasn't gone anywhere. If I sin, God isn't going to shut Himself off from me. But when I sin deliberately, I am no longer giving God all my attention. I am pushing Him aside to fulfil my own worldly desires. I am hiding from Him. By so doing, I am cheating myself out of the joy of being in constant fellowship with Jesus.

Consequently, I don't believe that God withholds miracles from me or refuses to engage in conversation with me when I sin. While some miracles may seem to require my complete faith in God for Him to perform them, I recognise that I have been the recipient of countless miracles even when I haven't had the faith to believe that they would happen.

When I draw away from God, however, I metaphorically cut the phone line between us. I may not even dare to ask Him for a miracle, because I believe the connection has been lost.

Conversely, when I am in complete fellowship with Jesus, I actually expect Him to act miraculously.

People seem to be quick to agree with the more popular attributes of God such as love, grace and forgiveness. In my experience, however, God's holiness is a stumbling block. The question we often hear is, "How could a loving God allow anyone to go to Hell?"

Interestingly, the Basis of Union of the Uniting Church in Australia allows for two opposing views about the nature of grace. The Uniting Church came about through the merging of the Congregational and Presbyterian churches (which embraced Calvinism) and the Methodist church (which had a strong Arminian tradition). So they had to allow for both views regarding grace.

1. The Arminian theology that was embraced by the Wesleys holds that grace is conditional upon the believer's *remaining in Christ*. Adherents of that theology hold that *"salvation is conditioned on faith, therefore perseverance is also conditioned"*[7].
2. The Calvinist theology says that it is only through accepting what Jesus did for us when He died on the Cross that we can be granted eternal life. There is an arm of this theology, however, which believes that because God loves all people, He won't choose some for salvation and others for damnation.

****

The "Omnis"

Do you put human limits on God? Let me assure you – as I said earlier in this chapter – that He is an *infinite* Being! Let's look again at these characteristics of God, which we can't even begin to comprehend except in the context of infinity.

His Omniscience

God is *omniscient*: He knows absolutely everything. He even knows how many hairs are on your head, and how many grains of sand are on the world's beaches. This is a great comfort to us, because it makes us realise that God knows exactly what we're going through.

His Omnipresence

God is *omnipresent*: He is everywhere at once. You don't need to say, "God has a Universe to run, and there are many people who need His help more than I do." If, as I said above, God knows how many grains of sand are

---

[7] Wikipedia: "Prevenient Grace (Arminianism)"

on the beach and how many hairs you have on your head, He must be everywhere at once.

His Omnipotence

God is *omnipotent*: His power is unlimited. God can do everything, but with one exception: He cannot go against His own character. That said, you can trust God to protect you in every situation. You can trust Him to provide miracles specifically for you. Contrary to Einstein's perception of God's Laws, they are not immutable. God can overrule them at any time, and for any purpose.

His Love

God is *love*: He doesn't just love; He is the *very definition* of love. We have seen evidence of that throughout the Bible, but none more so than in the fact that He gave His dear Son, Jesus, to pay the penalty for us. It's not that we love Him, but that He loves us – warts and all!

God's love is also infinite. He loves you personally as if you were the only person He created. I have to admit, however, that this is something I have never been able to get my head around. Even though Jesus demonstrated that love in what I suppose we can call a *human* way when He was here on Earth, it just seems too amazing that the God of the Universe could have such love for me personally!

The Ten Commandments

What use are the Ten Commandments today?

The Ten Commandments were given to the people of Israel as God's standard for living. But God never expected His people to obey them. He knew that they couldn't live by the first one, *"You shall have no other gods before Me"* (Exodus 20:3), let alone the following nine. So what purpose did the Ten Commandments serve? I believe they were given to the Israelites principally to show them that they were powerless to obtain salvation through observance of them. There are actually 613 commandments in the Old Testament, and I find it astounding that churches have decided which of those 613 laws are necessary for salvation, and which ones are not 'convenient' to obey.

Moreover, their list of *essential* laws seems to change from generation to generation.

Jesus' birth in Bethlehem heralded the arrival of a New Covenant, which actually came into force upon His death. Where the Old Covenant had been one of law, the New Covenant was one of grace. Obedience of the Old Testament laws, particularly those set out in Leviticus, had never been achievable. That is why Jesus came to Earth as a man. That is why Jesus had to suffer the most horrible death. Sin had to have a penalty, and He bore it on our behalf.

That is not to say that the Law does not still have a purpose. If there were no laws, there would be no sin. If the road you are driving on has no speed limits, you can't be booked for speeding. God's laws simply highlight our sinfulness, and it is only through the recognition of the fact that we are sinners that we will be able to turn to Jesus for forgiveness. Most of us also want to improve ourselves over the course of our lives. Trying to obey many of the Bible's laws will help us grow into better people. For example, the second Commandment given by Jesus in Matthew 22:39 is to love our neighbour as ourselves. This is a worthy goal to aim for. But even more important is the First Commandment that Jesus quoted (in Matthew 22:37): *To love God with all our heart and soul and mind.* That is what will bring us into a Deep Personal Relationship (hereafter referred to as 'DPR') with Jesus!

But many Christians, possibly most, try to keep a foot in both camps. They acknowledge that it is by grace they have been saved, but seem to think that they have to still obey the law if they are to keep in God's favour. Instead, they are effectively throwing Jesus' sacrifice out the window, replacing it with their own good works. But you can't be saved by works.

I truly believe that we miss out on so many of God's blessings for us, particularly His peace, because we think we have to obey His laws in order to keep in His good books. This is what Jesus was talking about when He spoke of sewing unshrunk cloth on an old garment, and of pouring new wine into old wineskins. As I explain in O, the results in both cases are disastrous.

"No one sews a patch of unshrunk cloth on an old garment. Otherwise, the new piece will pull away from the old, making the tear worse. And no one pours new wine into old wineskins. Otherwise, the wine will burst the skins,

and both the wine and the wineskins will be ruined. No, they pour new wine into new wineskins" (Mark 2:21-22).

The old garment and the old wineskins represent the Old Covenant of the law. The new ones represent the New Covenant of grace. I believe that millions of Christians throughout the world are missing out on the constant joy and peace they should be experiencing as forgiven children of God, simply because they think that their continued acceptance by God is dependent upon their following the old laws.

So when the Church tells me that my acceptance of Jesus as my Saviour is not enough, and that I have to repent of my homosexuality if God is to let me into His Heaven, it is making a grave error. It is mixing the law with grace, thereby misleading the whole world about what it means to be a Christian.

I mentioned in my Prologue the song **Amazing Grace**, which was written by John Newton in 1779, some years after he had cried out to God to save him while at sea in a violent storm. Like Newton, I discovered for myself that amazing grace in October 1977. It suddenly struck me that I didn't need to earn a ticket to Heaven. Jesus had already bought it for me. I am constantly amazed that God loves me. Whenever I hear **Amazing Grace** I marvel that God would even want to save *a wretch like me*.

Sadly, there are many Christians who still believe that God's acceptance of them is dependent upon their doing good. Sadly, there are many Christians who still believe that there are certain sins that will cause us to lose our salvation. Some of my own Christian friends have told me that I will lose my salvation if I don't repent of my homosexuality. I believe those people have misunderstood the finality of Jesus' sacrifice on the cross. To me it is a sign of disrespect for what He has done for us.

Have you heard people who don't attend church say that they try to follow the Ten Commandments? Of course they don't really try. They've been disqualified by the first one – *"You shall have no other gods before Me"* (Exodus 20:3) – and probably the other nine. But what I find most sad about this common declaration is that it reveals a world which is totally unaware that Jesus' death ushered in a completely new covenant, one where grace has superseded observance of the 'law'.

Grace

For it is by grace you have been saved, through faith – and this not from yourselves, it is the gift of God – not by works, so that no one can boast.
Ephesians 2:8-9

As far as the east is from the west, so far has He removed our transgressions from us.
Psalm 103:12

Amazing grace – amazing love

Linda Washington's message in ***Our Daily Bread*** on 15 August 2017 was based on Psalm 91:4, which says *"He will cover you with His feathers, and under His wings you will find refuge"*. Linda went on to say, *"When fear causes hope to fade, flee to God, the refuge you can reach on your knees!"*

Turn to God, trusting that when you don't understand why you are suffering, the life He has already given you, even in its pain, is still beautiful and good.

"The boundary lines have fallen for me in pleasant places; surely I have a delightful inheritance. I will praise the Lord, who counsels me; even at night my heart instructs me. I keep my eyes always on the Lord. With him at my right hand, I will not be shaken" (Psalm 16:6-8).

Monica Brands wrote in ***Our Daily Bread*** on 8 February 2019: *"And we can surrender to His loving arms that tenderly carry us through our pain into a peace and joy that even death can never quench"*.

God cannot go against His own nature. While He loves every one of us, His holiness would be compromised if He allowed unforgiven sinful people into Heaven. God put the sin of all mankind onto Jesus' shoulders, thus making perfect anyone who asks Jesus for forgiveness. Simply put: Grace is Jesus.

God and Gays

How do I know that God does not condemn me for being gay?

He has told me many times that He has blessed my marriage to Chan. To think that He would bless a same-sex union in the same way He blesses a heterosexual one might be a shock to you, but I believe it will become clear once you develop a DPR with Him.

Secondly, I was born gay. Some people still seem to think that homosexuality is a choice. If God made me gay, how could He condemn me for it? Even if you don't believe that God made me gay, you have to agree that He knew I would turn out gay: *"Before I formed you in the womb I knew you, before you were born I set you apart"* (Jeremiah 1:5). Even Pope Francis, addressing a gay man, said, *"God made you this way and loves you this way, and it doesn't matter to me"*[8].

Finally, and most importantly, <u>God sees me as His perfect child</u>, because Jesus made me perfect through His death on the cross.

I can't imagine what it would have been like to be a leper 2,000 years ago. Lepers were forbidden physical contact with any other human being (other than fellow lepers), including their own families, as this horrible disease slowly ravished their bodies, resulting in a slow and painful death. But I imagine that the ostracism from their loved ones and their communities would have been the worst thing about the disease.

Gay people believe that as God's representatives on Earth, Christians are speaking for Him when they say that homosexuality is abhorrent to Him.

Very much like the lepers!

But even if I'm gay, doesn't God condemn gay sex? This is a tricky question, and one that Christians the world over cannot agree on. If God does indeed regard homosexual practice as abhorrent, what about divorce, abortion, women's submission to their husbands, covetousness, and so on? As I have said elsewhere, Jesus condemned divorce, but made no mention of homosexual practice.

The Bible clearly says that we were made for relationship, not just with God, but also at a temporal level. After all, when God created Adam, He said, *"It is not good for the man to be alone"* (Genesis 2:18). Why can't I enjoy an intimate relationship with the man I love?

---

[8] *The Sydney Morning Herald*, 23 May 2018.

****

Christian missionaries have long sacrificed their comfort and safety in an attempt to introduce Jesus to people in Third World countries. When we think of missionaries, we remember those great men and women who made – and continue to make – amazing sacrifices for the Gospel. But we have an equally needy mission field right where we live. If you're a Christian, you have a duty to be a missionary somewhere. That may be in darkest Africa, but it is more likely to be exactly where you are right now. There are people in your sphere of influence who need to hear the Good News of eternal life through Jesus. Perhaps they're heterosexual non-Christians; perhaps they even go to church and think that makes them Christian; perhaps they are gay and steer clear of anything *religious*.

Don't take the risk that you might see your neighbour queued up to face God on Judgement Day, and he or she says to you, "Why didn't you tell me?"

Gay Christian Artists

There are quite a few well-known Christian singers and songwriters who have come out as gay in recent years. In the past, they had to keep it secret, so for some it was only after their deaths that they were revealed to have been gay. Some, though, bare their souls in post-coming-out songs.

Jim Nabors

I used to love watching **Gomer Pyle, USMC** on TV in the 1960s. It was a spin-off from the well-known **Andy Griffith Show**, which was where the character Gomer Pyle was created. Nabors was very funny in those shows, but he was also a gifted singer, recording quite a few albums. And he was a committed Christian.

What the wider world didn't know back in those days was that Jim Nabors was gay. He had been with his partner, Stan Cadwallader, for 38 years when they finally married in 2013, a month after same-sex marriage became legal in the US. By then, Nabors was 82 years old.

How sad that a couple who clearly loved each other had to keep that love secret from the world for so long.

Ray Boltz

Ray Boltz is an amazing man of God, whose Christian songs have had a huge impact on worship. After many years living a heterosexual lifestyle, with a wife and four children, Ray finally came out as gay. His contract with his recording studio was immediately terminated. One vindictive man wrote afterwards that Ray could no longer sing what was probably his most successful song, **I Pledge Allegiance to the Lamb**, as if acknowledging publicly that he was gay had somehow severed his relationship with Jesus. Boltz's *coming out* album, called **True**, was particularly inspiring to me. Incidentally, Ray's now ex-wife, Carol, continued to support him, even joining the Board of the gay Christian organisation, **Soulforce**.

Trey Pearson

Trey Pearson, like Ray Boltz and me, finally admitted – while being in a heterosexual marriage, and with two children – that he was gay. But, as a musician in a Christian rock band, Pearson faced another issue. After announcing how pleased he was to be *"the first openly gay artist to ever play at a major Christian music festival"*, he was forced to drop out of the planned concert, **Joshua Fest**. Yet, in a display of true Christian forgiveness, he had no bitterness towards the people who had forced him out.

Some time after his coming out, Trey wrote an amazing song, titled **Hey Jesus**, in which he asks Jesus if He still loves him now that he's come out as gay.

Only One Way

Jesus answered, 'I am the way and the truth and the life. No one comes to the Father except through Me'.
John 14:6

I was shocked and dismayed to read an article in a Christian publication[9] in October 2021 that spoke of a recent study in the United States where it was found that *"almost 70 percent of born-again Christians say Jesus Christ isn't the only way to God"*. The survey involved *"3,106 Americans aged 18 to 55 from all religious groups, including 717 respondents who identify as born-*

---

[9] Article by Milton Quintanilla in **ChristianHeadlines.com** on 22 October 2021

again Christians". I wonder what the concept *born again* means to those people. To refer to themselves as 'born again', they must have realised that they were 'dead' in the first place. So what saved them?

Society today believes that we should be broad-minded regarding just about every issue. People generally believe that Christians are arrogant to assert that Jesus is the only way to Heaven. But Jesus stated very clearly that He *is* the only way to Heaven.

When I was a small boy, we used to play hide-and-seek, as I imagine just about every child did at some stage. I was always amazed, though, when one of the other kids would simply close their eyes, presumably reasoning that, if they could not see the one who was 'in', they couldn't be seen either. Sadly, too many adults still play that game. They figure that closing their eyes to the truth of God's message will make it go away. It won't.

Josh McDowell wrote in his famous book, **More than a Carpenter**[10], that Jesus presented Himself as *"the only avenue to a relationship with God, the only source of forgiveness for sins, and the only way of salvation. For many people, this is too exclusive, too narrow for them to want to believe. Yet the issue is not what do we want to think or believe, but rather, who did Jesus claim to be?"*

We had a really hot youth worker (and I'm speaking as a gay man here!) at our Anglican church in Sydney's northern suburb of Avalon Beach in the early 1980s. Gordon Barnes, who had been a champion surfer before taking on the role of youth pastor at our church, used to preach in the evening services to the young members of our congregation. But I remember clearly a sermon he gave to the older generation one Sunday morning which illustrated my belief that no one can find God without first finding Jesus. This is as close as I can remember to his words:

> It's a sunny day. Let's imagine that we all walk out of the church, cross the road to the beach and start swimming to New Zealand. Some of you won't make it past the breakers. Others will cover quite a distance. I will probably get further than any of you. But none of us will make it. We're simply not

---

[10] ©1977, Josh McDowell

good enough swimmers to cross the Tasman. In the same way, we can never be good enough to make it to Heaven under our own steam.

John North wrote in **Time with God** on 8 October 2019:

> There is only one way to a wonderful eternity with God and that is through the person of Jesus Christ! If there was any other way for a person to become acceptable to God, you can be sure God would have taken that other way. No one can ever measure the pain to the heart of God the Son to take on Himself the sin and guilt of the whole world, or the pain in the heart of God the Father as He turned away, for the first time in all eternity, from His dear Son because of the sin of the world. No, God wants you to know that if He could find no other way, then neither can you. But how He longs for you to take the way He has provided at such a great cost. He wants you to be with Him for all eternity.

I believe that without Jesus in their lives, people can't be truly at peace. God created a vacuum in us that cannot be filled other than by Jesus. I was interested in the following comment by Dr Andrew Weil in a magazine[11] in 2019:

> An American Psychiatric Association poll in 2017 found that nearly two-thirds of Americans were *extremely or somewhat anxious* and more than a third were more anxious overall than in the previous year. Depression, which often accompanies anxiety, is both an American and a global epidemic, with the World Health Organization reporting that it has recently become the world's leading cause of disability.

What Does God Intend for Us?

Everlasting life

Yet to all who did receive Him, to those who believed in His name, He gave the right to become children of God.
John 1:12

When God created Adam and Eve, the Garden of Eden was Utopia. The plan was that all His people would have everlasting life, with no sickness, pain or death. Mankind was to live in perfect fellowship with God and, in fact, that

---

[11] **Seabourn Herald** Volume 29 Number 2

is exactly how it was in the beginning. However, once Satan had succeeded in tempting Adam and Eve to eat the forbidden fruit, 100 per cent of the world's then-population – all two of them – were damned, along with everyone else born since then.

But God did not want the whole world to be lost. After all, He had made us in His own image (except for the sin bit). He gave us choice, so that we wouldn't just be His puppets. But Adam and Eve blew it. And then we all blew it.

That is why Jesus had to come down from Heaven to pay the price for our sinfulness. He wanted to restore us into God's likeness, perfect in His sight.

I now have everlasting life, as do you if you have received Jesus as your Saviour. It sounds paradoxical but, while my life is now more joyful than it has ever been, I can't wait to get to Heaven. When that happens, I will literally be able to walk side-by-side with Jesus in the garden. To be in His physical presence has got to be far better than anything we can ever imagine happening to us here.

Most Christians have heard of, and have great respect for, Charles Spurgeon. Known as the *Prince of Preachers* in the 19th century, as well as being a prolific author, Spurgeon once said:

> Depend upon it, your dying hour will be the best hour you have ever known[12]! Your last moment will be your richest moment, better than the day of your birth will be the day of your death. It shall be the beginning of Heaven, the rising of the sun that shall go no more down forever.

Perfect fellowship with Him

"Here I am! I stand at the door and knock. If anyone hears My voice and opens the door, I will come in and eat with that person, and they with Me" (Revelation 3:20).

Do you know the Parable of the Lost (or Prodigal) Son, as explained by Jesus in Luke 15:11-32? I believe the story is actually more about the father than the son. While the son went off to squander his inheritance, which his father had graciously given him in advance of his own death, the father waited

---

[12] From Ecclesiastes 7:1

anxiously on the front doorstep for him to come home again. When the son finally did return to his father, full of remorse for his foolishness, did the father say, *"I told you so; now you come back home begging for help."*? No, he rushed to the front gate and wrapped his son in a bear hug, lavishing him with kisses. That man was a representation of our own heavenly Father, who pleads with us to return to Him.

Before the fall, Adam and Eve lived in perfect fellowship with God. Genesis 3:8 tells us that God was in the habit of *"walking in the garden in the cool of the day"* with Adam and Eve. But after their sin, they were too embarrassed for God to see them, so *"they hid from the Lord God among the trees of the garden"*. This is exactly what we have done. Perhaps unconsciously aware of our own sinfulness, we have hidden from God. I believe this is one of the reasons people won't even explore the possibility of entering into a relationship with Him.

Not only that, but I have realised after talking with non-Christian friends that they don't think of God as a *person*, but as a *higher power*. It's no wonder that the concept of a relationship with our Creator is so foreign to them.

Jesus is with me all the time. He even accompanies me when I go for my morning run around our neighbourhood. He frequently makes me chuckle aloud at something He has revealed to me. I'm chuckling even as I write this. But am I in perfect fellowship with Him? Sadly, no. Like you, sometimes I turn from Him in search of my own pleasure. Then I go and hide from Him *"among the trees of the garden"*.

Most of the time, however, I have awesome fellowship with Jesus; enough to make me yearn for perfect fellowship with Him for eternity.

****

Dr Charles Stanley, who produces a daily devotional message from his **In Touch Ministries**, wrote the following one titled ***Two Gates, Two Ways***:

> Have you ever been accused of being a narrow-minded Christian? Those who level such accusations against us certainly mean it as an insult. According to Jesus, however, that's the only way to walk if we want to experience abundant life now and eternal life with Him in Heaven. But it will require a deliberate choice on our part, because no one automatically drifts onto this pathway.

The broad way is easy to find. In fact, unless you make a conscious choice to avoid it, you'll find yourself on it. Most people like this wide path because it encompasses all philosophies and belief systems. Everything is acceptable, and everyone's 'truth' is valid. It even seems like the loving path because no one is left out. There are no restrictions, and freedom is unlimited. Or is it?

****

I have been told that I can't be a Christian if I continue to sin deliberately. But that's the same for every one of us. If such a warning were true, Heaven would be empty! In fact, the Bible contains countless stories of people who failed God in this way.

King David had an affair with Bathsheba, making her pregnant. He then had her husband murdered in an attempt to hide his wrongdoing. Yet God, who would certainly have known what heinous sin David was soon to commit, had a little earlier described David as *"a man after His own heart"* (1 Samuel 13:14; Acts 13:22). As I say in Chapter 3, David is my Old Testament hero.

Incidentally, there have been a lot of 'David and Bathsheba' incidents in Pentecostal churches in recent times. A number of pastors, who have worked tirelessly for God's Kingdom for years, have been unceremoniously dumped from their roles when they've been caught out on the sin of adultery. How many Pentecostal pastors do you know of who are 'squeaky clean'? It may not be an adulterous affair. Perhaps it is the sin of greed (which seems to be prevalent among that community!). Yet God continues to use them mightily, just as He did with David.

Anthony Venn-Brown was one such pastor who lost his ministry. Before he was forced to leave the **Assemblies of God** church in 1992, having admitted to the leadership that he had had sex with another man, Anthony did a simply amazing job in reaching young people for Jesus. Through his organisation, **Every Believer Evangelism**, Anthony created a ministry aimed at the young, titled **Youth Alive**. Countless young people have been saved by this ministry, which continues to this day. Yet the Church, having deemed Anthony's sin to be greater than the sins the church leadership were committing, put an immediate stop to his ministry. Satan must have rubbed his hands in glee at this.

Paul, one of the godliest people who have ever lived, also struggled with sin. *"We know that the law is spiritual; but I am unspiritual, sold as a slave to* sin. I do not understand what I do. For what I want to do I do not do, but what I hate I do. And if I do what I do not want to do, I agree that the law is good. As it is, it is no longer I myself who does it, but it is sin living in me. For I know that good itself does not dwell in me, that is, in my sinful nature. For I have the desire to do what is good, but I cannot carry it out. For I do not do the good I want to do, but the evil I do not want to do – this I keep on doing"* (Romans 7:14-19).

I am now learning to trust not in my faith, but in Jesus Himself. There's a subtle difference between the two, which probably needs some explanation.

For example, I believe the Bible gives good advice in avoiding temptation, warning us to dismiss an unhealthy or evil desire from our minds before it can take root.

"...each person is tempted when they are dragged away by their own evil desire and enticed. Then, after desire has conceived, it gives birth to sin; and sin, when it is full-grown, gives birth to death" (James 1:14-15).

"My grace is sufficient for you, for My power is made perfect in weakness" (2 Corinthians 12:9).

So I've found that having faith to believe something is possible is not enough. But I do have faith to believe that Jesus loves me, and that He can take control over any situation. It's actually His faith, not mine, that comes into play.

****

This brings me to **Qarah**.

Qarah

I am normally sceptical of the motives of pastors of so-called megachurches, of which there is an ever-increasing number. But not all of them have been tainted by fame and fortune. Joseph Prince is one such person. My husband and I have had the privilege of attending quite a few services at his **New Creation Church** in Singapore in recent times. As the Senior Pastor at his church of 35,000 people, Prince preaches nothing but Jesus' grace to those of us who will accept Him as our Saviour. He has a gift of discernment, enabling him to interpret the Bible in a way that really brings the Word of God to life.

I subscribe to Joseph Prince's daily devotionals, where he often talks about *qarah*[13], a word used in some versions of the Bible, and which can loosely be described as *positioning for good success*. It is something I ask God for every morning, before I even get out of bed.

Here's just one example of how *qarah* plays out, although this one is a little more dramatic than usual:

Visiting a dear friend at John James Hospital in Canberra one afternoon in January 2017, I noticed after an hour or so that the sky was turning black, and thought I should leave quickly so that I could get to my car before it rained. Jenny was enjoying my visit so much, though, that I stayed another 15 minutes. Here is what I wrote the next day in my diary: *"After praying for Jenny, I had to run through moderate rain to get to my car, regretting that I hadn't left a bit earlier. Had I left when I'd intended, I would have been caught in the middle of a sudden, violent and unexpected storm. Trees had been uprooted ... and countless cars were damaged or even destroyed. But when I came through ... all was still!"*. My daily prayer for *Qarah* had been answered!

I then wrote:

> *"God will make a way, when there seems to be no way"*. As I listened to the radio while moving slowly along Northbourne Avenue, it was reported that the road was closed in both directions, with trees strewn across both carriageways. There were also reports that traffic lights were out right across the city. Yet, despite the fact that emergency services hadn't yet arrived (although a solitary police car had parked at one point on the side of the road), the northbound carriageway was clear as I drove through! Speaking to Kari [my sister] on the phone as I was driving, I told her that there was no wind or rain. She said I was probably in the eye of the storm, and that I could expect to feel its full force shortly. I told her confidently that I believed God was protecting me and that I had nothing to fear. I could sense her scepticism at that!

---

[13] This comes from Genesis 24:12 (and many other verses). While *qarah* is an ancient Hebrew word, it is usually translated in Bibles these days as 'success'. I like the word *qarah*, as it encompasses the action of 'positioning for good success'. In other words, it's rather like *serendipity*, though in the case of *qarah* it is not merely chance that brings success, but is something that has been orchestrated by God.

In case I had been tempted to think that the miracle of protection from the storm had been a coincidence, my first devotional the next day[14], by Mart DeHaan, was titled ***Growing in the Wind***, and was based on Mark 4:41:

"Who is this? Even the wind and the waves obey Him!"

Mart made another interesting observation in that devotional: *"... how strong would our faith be if we couldn't discover for ourselves His reassuring 'be still' when the winds of circumstances howl?"* That was certainly another faith-building experience for me.

---

[14] ***Our Daily Bread***, 14 January 2017

CHAPTER 2

Man

Be perfect, therefore, as your heavenly Father is perfect.
Matthew 5:48

We Are All Sinners

In his letter to the Romans, Paul made clear our wretched state before God. *"For all have sinned and fall short of the glory of God"* (Romans 3:23). He then made an amazing pronouncement: *"For the wages of sin is death, but the gift of God is eternal life in Christ Jesus our Lord"* (Romans 6:23).

Paul acknowledged that we could never earn our way into Heaven. Until his miraculous conversion on the road to Damascus, Saul (as his name was then) had dedicated his life to eradicating the new Christian movement, whose radical beliefs about salvation through grace did not sit well with his own commitment to following the Law to achieve salvation.

What Has Happened in the Last 2,000 Years?

The world has changed since Jesus trod this Earth, and probably ever since the time of Adam and Eve. And the changes seem to be gathering pace. What was unacceptable even fifty years ago is now accepted practice. For example, it was rare for an unmarried couple to live together when I was a youngster.

Now it seems to be the norm, often with no intention of 'buying the goods after testing them out'. God warned Moses more than 3,000 years ago, what would happen to a society that allowed unacceptable practices:

"Do not degrade your daughter by making her a prostitute, or the land will turn to prostitution and be filled with wickedness" (Leviticus 19:29).

Homosexuality did not exist at the beginning, although there are many accounts of prominent people – particularly Roman and Greek army leaders – who were living in openly gay relationships by the time Jesus came on the scene. *My opinion is that because of sinful choices made over the centuries, some of us are now born gay.* Not only is it acceptable to secular society, but those of us who are gay know that it was not of our choosing to be this way. It has become obvious to us that most of us, if not all of us, were *born* gay.

Charles Stanley made the following interesting observation in one of his daily devotionals about the effect of Adam and Eve's sin:

> That first rebellion plunged humanity into a terrible condition. Civilisation is now plagued by countless ramifications of the innumerable sins committed by human beings throughout the ages. Is it any wonder the world is in such sad shape? Sin not only causes suffering: It robs us of God's best. The Garden of Eden is closed and locked to sinful mankind.

CS Lewis, whom I mentioned earlier, also made an interesting observation in **Mere Christianity**: That it is *"the Christian view that this is a good world that has gone wrong, but still retains the memory of what ought to have been"*.

Jesus died about 2,000 years ago, and I believe that mankind has been moving further away from Him ever since. But now it has reached a critical point. Even in my own lifetime I've seen a huge change. Where in the 1950s there was no sport played in Australia on Sundays, and most people attended church, we have now made Sunday like any other day. I'm not going to argue against that here. I am just pointing out that we've replaced God with idols of our own making.

It's interesting how our understanding of the Bible has changed over those two millennia. Christians used the Bible to justify slavery for most of that period. They have used it to justify discrimination against people of colour. It's only recently that women have even been allowed to speak in church, let alone preach there[15]. And it is still being used by Christians the world over to condemn homosexual practice and, in some cases, even homosexuals.

I don't believe that Christians ever wilfully sin, but I do believe that we *all* deliberately sin. I explain the difference between *wilful* and *deliberate* sin a little later in this chapter. This is why it is important to understand the Old Testament, and its role as a key element of the Bible. God doesn't expect us to obey the Ten Commandments – He knows we can't. What He wants us to know is that without Christ we are doomed.

That is not to say that we shouldn't try to obey the Ten Commandments to the best of our ability. The First Commandment, *"You shall have no other gods before Me"* (Exodus 20:3), is something we should all aim for. But if it is something we will never attain, why should we even try? Because God wants us to have a DPR with Him, and the only way we can really do that is if we let go of the other gods that compete for our attention. As I have said many times in this book, there is absolutely nothing better in life than having a DPR with Jesus! Those Commandments are there for *our* benefit, not God's.

I want to stress that the Old Testament is still extremely useful for Christians today. Not only has it shown us that we can never measure up to God's standard, as set out in His laws, but the experiences of the Old Testament characters are a real inspiration to us. As I wrote earlier, David was described by God as *"a man after My own heart"* (Acts 13:22), despite the fact that he committed some atrocious sins. How inspiring is that!

But we do need to study the Old Testament from a New Testament perspective. Its laws are no longer a prerequisite to salvation, and we need to remember that Jesus did away with that requirement when He sacrificed His life on the cross. While the most important commandments (as stated by Jesus in Matthew 22:37-40, and which I talk more about in Chapter 4) are goals to aspire to, most of the civil commandments no longer apply. The banning of pork from the diet of the Israelites, for example, was for valid health reasons. But today, with health protocols ensuring that pork is not dangerous to eat, the rationale for that restriction no longer applies, although the tradition continues with Jewish and Muslim people. Jesus Himself said, *"What goes into*

---

[15] Some churches still ban women from being ordained, and even from preaching.

someone's mouth does not defile them, but what comes out of their mouth, that is what defiles them".(Matthew 15:11).

I think the usefulness of the Ten Commandments today is in showing us what living in Christ really means. Once you have a DPR with Jesus, you will display the 'fruit of the Spirit', which actually covers everything that the Law may have tried to instil into you. *"But the fruit of the Spirit is love, joy, peace, forbearance [patience], kindness, goodness, faithfulness, gentleness and self-control. Against such things there is no law"* (Galatians 5:22-23).

Wilful versus Deliberate Sin

Come on, admit it! You've done some bad things in your life. So have I. Do I continue to sin deliberately[16]? Yes. Do I continue to sin wilfully[17]? No. I love the Lord so much that it probably seems inconceivable that I would deliberately choose to sin. But, while God sees me as perfect now, I am still living in a fallen world, and I still have my human weaknesses and failings.

But I don't sin wilfully. Before I became a Christian, cheating the Tax Man was considered a sport in business circles, and I was caught up in that. In fact, it didn't even occur to me that having a tax-free expense account might be wrong. In the heady days of the 1970s – well before Australia introduced the Fringe Benefits Tax in 1986 – there was no such thing as 'self-assessment' for tax. If you were doing something wrong, it was up to the Tax Man to find it. Otherwise, anything was fair game.

Why is there a distinction between *deliberate* and *wilful* sin? I believe that Christians are constrained by the Holy Spirit when they sin. They might continue to sin deliberately, but they know it's not something that would please God. In fact, I believe that cheating on your tax, for example, simply shows a lack of faith. It's saying to God that you don't trust Him for all your needs.

The most important thing to remember, however, is that God still sees me as perfect. One of my favourite songs is **We Must Remember**, by Jeremy Camp. Again, I'm reminded of Hebrews 8:12:*"For I will forgive their wickedness and will remember their sins no more"*. Here is the first verse of the song:

---

[16] That is, 'consciously and intentionally'.

[17] That is, 'with a desire to sin'.

> We must remember
> That You have forgotten
> And You don't remember our sins any more.
> We must remember
> That You have forgotten
> And You, You died once and for all.

I am grateful that God does see me as perfect now. Otherwise, I would be perpetually on my knees! Jesus paid the penalty for my sins 2,000 years before I was born, so at that time they were *all* in the future. It was a once-only payment. I don't need to ask for His forgiveness every time I sin. Like you, I commit the ongoing sin of failing to love God above everything else.

Does God really love you?

I became a Christian in 1977, and I now have the most wonderful DPR with the Lord Jesus Christ. I am also gay, and it was a long time before I realised that not only does God love me as I am, but I have no doubt at all that He actually created me this way. I also know that Jesus *likes* me and loves to *hang out* with me. Can you identify with that? If so, do you think that Jesus would like you, but not me, based only on my sexuality? Importantly, being homosexual is not a choice. It just *is*. Since coming out in 2003 at the age of 54 I have not met a gay person who would have chosen to be gay. Similarly, the lepers in Jesus' day did not choose to be ill, nor to be ostracised from their communities. Sadly it is not very different for gay people today, where in some communities they are still considered to be outcasts, simply for being born 'different'.

Homosexual practice is, on the other hand, a choice. In gathering material for this book, I realised that the Church and the gay community are unlikely to agree on the acceptability of living a 'gay lifestyle', at least in my lifetime. But that is not the critical point. It is *grace* that matters. People ask me how I can be so sure that I will go to Heaven when I die. You can be assured from God's Word that all Christians have the promise of eternal life. John said, *"I write these things to you who believe in the name of the Son of God so that you may know that you have eternal life"* (1 John 5:13).

One of the two criminals who were crucified alongside Jesus acknowledged his sinfulness right at the end, and realised that Jesus was paying the penalty for the sins of mankind, not for His own sins. Jesus said to him: *"Truly I tell you, today you will be with Me in Paradise"* (Luke 23:43). In other words, *"You have accepted Me as your Lord and Saviour, so your sins are forgiven, and you shall join Me in Heaven"*.

As I have been keen to point out, it is solely because of Jesus' death on the cross, and because I have invited Him into my life, that I can know for certain I will go to Heaven. Nothing I have done, or will do in the future, can change that truth.

I have been told by Christians, including clergy, that I may lose my salvation if I continue to sin, but that is simply wrong. I sin every day of my life, but God doesn't see that, because I have His grace. The Lord said, *"Though your sins are like scarlet, they shall be as white as snow"* (Isaiah 1:18).

My salvation is not dependent on me, but on Jesus. Once I invited Him into my life, I was given absolute assurance that God would never let me go. The contract is not between God and me, but between God and Jesus.

Some of my friends, sceptical about the life hereafter, have been tempted to ask me what will happen if I am wrong about Heaven and Hell. But of course my DPR with Jesus has given me absolute assurance that I am not wrong in my understanding of what will happen when I die, and that my future in Heaven is secure. I have my ticket, and my bags are packed. For the sake of argument, however, if you think that my relationship with Jesus is possibly not real, I would say this: If I turn out to have been wrong about the existence of Heaven, perhaps I have missed out on some of life's pleasures; but if you're wrong, it doesn't bear thinking about.

Whose Are You?

As I said in the Foreword, God is not so concerned about who or what you are, but *whose* you are! It is insignificant to Him whether you are black or white, male or female, gay or straight. He just wants you to be *His*.

Some people I have met over the years have said that they can't come into God's presence, because their lives are in too much of a mess; that a holy God couldn't even look at someone like them. This is the crux of the issue with the gay community: The Church tells gays to 'clean themselves up', before it will allow them to worship God in their establishments. Even if the Church were correct that the Bible declares homosexuality a sin (which I believe it doesn't), how do people get the idea that we have to be clean *before* we have a bath? Jesus didn't ever tell anyone to clean themselves up before coming to Him for cleansing.

In 0 I explained my understanding of grace, and backed up my position with a number of relevant biblical quotes. Yet, despite the 'state of grace' being promulgated by many churches as the ideal, they seem to have forgotten that it is God who bestows grace and He doesn't require any payment for it, save that anyone seeking it must ask Jesus for forgiveness of their sins and accept Him as their Lord. The Old Testament *law* is another issue entirely, and the one fact from the Bible that I wish the Church would understand is the difference between the Old Testament *law* and the New Testament *grace*. *"For the law was given through Moses; grace and truth came through Jesus Christ"* (John 1:17).

I am righteous and my righteousness is a gift from God. Jesus said: *"The thief comes only to steal and kill and destroy; I have come that they may have life, and have it to the full"* (John 10:10). I was freed from the law when Jesus went to the cross, and because I asked Him for forgiveness. His grace is available to all.

What Is a Christian?

A Christian is, quite simply, someone who has recognised that they are a sinner by nature, and who has realised that Jesus alone can cleanse them of that sin. You do not become a Christian by being a 'good' person. You become a Christian through grace alone. *"For it is by grace you have been saved, through faith – and this not from yourselves, it is the gift of God – not by works, so that no one can boast"* (Ephesians 2:8-9).

The Roman Catholic Church does not believe that. That is why it can't call itself Christian, which I will expand on later.

CHAPTER 3

The Church

They have lost connection with the head, from whom the whole body, supported and held together by its ligaments and sinews, grows as God causes it to grow.
Colossians 2:19

Imagine you are a diplomat serving your country in one ruled by an oppressive regime. It is your duty to promote your own country at every opportunity. Instead, however, you extol the virtues of your host country. Christians are ambassadors, posted to this fallen world on behalf of our heavenly Father's Kingdom. But the Church has forgotten its role, and instead seems more intent on promoting a life bound by earthly rules, completely misrepresenting God's message to an oppressed people.

Too many churches are still living under the strict laws of the Old Testament. The New Covenant, ushered in by God's own precious Son, Jesus, is incredibly liberating. I am now the righteousness of Christ, and any Christian who doubts that has a problem understanding their own salvation.

Sadly, Satan has been all-too-successful in persuading church leaders that grace is not enough, though most of them probably would not realise that this is what they are conveying to their congregations – and many would deny it. They say that we have to strive to be good if we are to continue to be accepted by Jesus. He is not called the *accuser* for nothing. (His very name, *Satan,* means *accuser* in Hebrew.) Satan will take every opportunity to point out our faults, accusing us of failing as Christians: *"Call yourself a Christian? After what you've just done?"* Have you ever heard that accusation in your head and assumed it was your own thought? It was Satan doing what Satan does best: Undermining your confidence in God.

Just as he persuaded Eve to sin, <u>Satan has convinced the Church to accept flawed assumptions about God, by promoting unfounded doctrines and embracing heretical philosophies</u>. These are often not deliberate, but church leaders have become bound by traditions and the thought that 'this is what we have done for decades, so it must be right'. It suits Satan to have us bound by laws, and the Church has all-too-frequently fallen into his trap. Paul spoke in Galatians 5 about freedom in Christ, giving some very clear warnings to believers: *"It is for freedom that Christ has set us free. Stand firm, then, and do not let yourselves be burdened again by a yoke of slavery"* (verse 1); *"You who are trying to be justified by the law have been alienated from Christ; you have fallen away from grace"* (verse 4); *"You were running a good race. Who cut in on you to keep you from obeying the truth? That kind of persuasion does not come from the One who calls you"* (verses 7-8). Jesus Himself said, *"So if the Son sets you free, you will be free indeed"* (John 8:36).

In ***10 Real-Life Emotions Jesus Expressed***[18], Cindi McMenamin's succinct words expressed my own feelings about the Church:

> Do you feel anger toward leaders in the church and religious community who abuse their power, care more about their own comfort and image than that of other believers, and 'fleece the flock' in the name of service to God? Are you enraged by anyone who would, in the name of Christ or spirituality, lead other believers astray or interfere with the discipleship and growth of a new believer? Do you loathe legalism to the point of calling it what it is? Jesus did. And He made no apologies for such. Instead of being angry with sinners and how they lived, Jesus was indignant toward the so-called 'religious' who touted a spotless image on the outside, but cultivated critical, hardened hearts on the inside. Jesus used harsh words toward the religious elite of his day saying things like, *'You snakes! You brood of vipers! How will you escape being condemned to Hell?'* (Matthew 23:33).

Jesus was really angry when He arrived at the temple to find traders and money changers making themselves rich at the expense of the poor people who had come to make the obligatory sacrifice. Jesus went 'wild', if I can use

---

[18] Crosswalk, 24 May 2018

that adjective in respect of a member of the Godhead, overturning the money changers' tables and releasing all the sacrificial animals waiting to be sold. So why did Jesus get so angry? It was because the priests and others were using God's House to take advantage of the poor and make themselves rich. There was nothing 'noble' about what they were doing. And it's just the same today.

****

In **Gospel Transformation Notes**[19], the author speaks of John 2:13-22:

> In Israel's history, the temple represented God's gracious dwelling among his covenant people. By his own initiative, he provided for a restored relationship with his sinful people (Exodus 25:8–9). <u>Unfortunately, however, ritual replaced reality, and pride was more obvious than humility; the 'worship of worship' – and, as seen here, the desire for financial gain – took precedence over the worship of God</u> [my emphasis].

In too many churches today, nothing has changed!

Pre-Reformation Times

Martin Luther changed the world, if not the Roman Catholic Church. Before Luther translated the Bible from Latin into the German vernacular, thereby making it available to everyone to read, priests were regarded as the conduit between man and God. The Church was vehemently against the concept of laymen being able to go directly to God, claiming that only priests had the wisdom imparted by the Bible to allow discernment of His Word.

Of course this made it very easy for the Church to manipulate the masses. If the Church said that you had to pay *indulgences* to atone for your sins, who were you to argue? You didn't even have access to a Bible, and if you did, it was in Latin. The Church was very big on the importance of 'works', in order to gain or retain salvation.

Sadly, it seems we are still stuck in pre-Reformation times.

---

[19] © 2013 by Crossway

The Industrial Revolution

The Industrial Revolution, which began in England in the second half of the 18th century, changed the world forever. People moved from their little villages to the burgeoning towns and cities, capitalising on the new opportunities afforded even to the lower classes. The standard of living of the average person suddenly improved dramatically. No longer did people's lives revolve around the village church and a dependence on God. Capitalism brought with it a new god: Wealth, and the materialism it enabled. The masses were now masters of their own destiny – or so they thought.

What Drives Us – and the Church?

Most people are driven by either power or money, and often both. Some of the leaders of the more than 1,500 megachurches[20] in the United States alone have made names for themselves as movers and shakers in the Capitol.

Power

One of the better-known preachers in recent times is Paula White, who was Donald Trump's spiritual adviser and pastor when he occupied the White House. Although White wielded a lot of power in that position, it apparently did not extend to her influence over God! In November 2020, *"Paula White hosted an impassioned prayer service even as the election results were coming in and people on social media have since come up with memes and remixes of it. The pastor led a marathon prayer service at the New Christian Destiny Centre, calling for divine intervention in the presidential race. This included requests for prayers from Africa and South America to help Trump to win. 'I hear a sound of victory, the Lord says it is done', White said even as all counting*

---

[20] **Megachurches** are defined by the Hartford Institute for Religious Research as *"very active Protestant congregations with an average of 2,000 or more weekend attendees and a multitude of outreach programs and ministries"*.

indicated that Trump was trailing"[21]. At the time of writing, White had a personal net worth in excess of 7 million Australian dollars.

But the need for power goes well beyond the White House. Many megapastors in the United States have private jets, which they believe is a sign of God's favour on them. Kenneth Copeland, the richest pastor in America – and who will appear later in the book – purchased a top-level Gulfstream V. He announced to his followers on his ministry website in January 2018 that *"We have sown a GV as a team and God wants that kind of prosperity [for our team of 'Partners']"*. This was in addition to two other high-end aircraft!

What warped thinking makes a pastor suggest that God wants them to spend 100 million dollars or more on private jets, just so they can show He favours them? Do they really think that a private jet is proof of their power – that they are in the pocket of God?

Money

But godliness with contentment is great gain. For we brought nothing into the world, and we can take nothing out of it. But if we have food and clothing, we will be content with that. Those who want to get rich fall into temptation and a trap and into many foolish and harmful desires that plunge people into ruin and destruction. For the love of money is a root of all kinds of evil. Some people, eager for money, have wandered from the faith and pierced themselves with many griefs.
1 Timothy 6:6-10

I have found that Pentecostal churches in particular are reluctant to reveal a lot of financial information. Sure, they have to comply with Accounting Standards, at least in Australia. But those statutory financial reports don't reveal the full picture.

For example, the 2019 published financial report for a Pentecostal church in Canberra stated that 'key management personnel compensation' amounted to $183,158. Yet 'employee expenses' for the same year amounted to $650,908. There was no mention that the remuneration of the senior pastor's wife, who was clearly a member of the management team (and who was

---

[21] ***The Indian Express***, 28 January 2021

also referred to as a 'senior pastor'), was included; nor was there any indication that she was actually regarded as 'key management personnel' for the purposes of the document. There was an office secretary, but no indication of any other staff, although there was possibly a cleaner as well. In other words, there was an amount of $467,750 unaccounted for.

I believe all churches should have to provide specific and detailed accounts of their expenditure, including domestic and international travel costs for each person. Untaxed amounts should also be specified. How much of the pastor's remuneration, for example, is paid in the form of a tax-free fringe benefit?

Why does this concern me? As with anyone, I believe that church leaders can be tempted to fall into the 'money trap', unless they are fully accountable to the people they serve. In addition, because registered religious institutions enjoy special tax privileges – including unlimited[22] tax-free benefits for 'religious practitioners' – they should be subject to additional scrutiny.

Joel Osteen runs the biggest church in the US. He also owns an Airbus A319, which apparently cost 86 million US dollars. Osteen claimed in 2011 that apologising for being rich was 'almost an insult to our God'.

Sure, God lets some people become rich. But I believe that, as with all the 'talents' He gives His people, those who are financially blessed are charged with using their money to help the needy of the world – not to feather their own nests with numerous multi-million-dollar assets.

False Prophets

Dr Roger Barrier

Roger Barrier contributes a regular column to *Crosswalk*, and generally provides very godly counsel to his readers. But in **8 Things You Should Know about Gay Marriage**, which appeared in *Crosswalk* on 28 January 2021,

---

[22] While there is nothing to stop the church from providing 100% of a religious practitioner's remuneration tax-free, churches generally recommend limiting such benefits to a maximum of 75% of the remuneration package.

Roger made a serious error. While he states that *"Scientific research is producing more evidence that the gay attraction may very well be hard wired into both the anatomical and chemical makeup of some brains"*, Roger seems to believe that God condemns gay people if they act out on what is to them their natural sexual instinct. He says: *"Don't get me wrong. Homosexual behaviour is a sin at any level ... <u>No one can close the spiritual gap from where they are to an intimate relationship with Jesus Christ while acting out homosexual behaviour</u>"*.

That statement is absolutely false. I challenge Roger to disprove my DPR with Jesus, who has assured me over and over that I am His adored child – and that my homosexuality has absolutely no influence over our relationship.

Incidentally, Roger and I have since communicated, and I have found him to be a most gracious person, willing to be 'enlightened'. But he is still wrong on the subject of homosexuality.

'Prosperity Gospel' Teachers

The so-called *Prosperity Gospel* is alive and well, particularly within Pentecostal churches. Too many of their pastors use the Bible to justify their own wealth, assuring us that God wants us all to be rich. But God tells His people what their money is for: *"... that they may have something to share with those in need"* (Ephesians 4:28). Despite what people may tell you about the benefits of being rich, it is a close relationship with God, rather than what He can do for you, that will give meaning and pleasure to your life.

There is a verse in the Bible that Prosperity Gospel protagonists rely on to justify their self-serving insistence that God wants them to be wealthy. Jeremiah 29:11 says, *"'For I know the plans I have for you', declares the Lord, 'plans to prosper you and not to harm you, plans to give you a hope and a future'"*.

I don't believe that the word 'prosper' in that verse refers to financial wealth, but to success in life. Success should never be measured in terms of a person's bank account. God requires us to focus on service to Him and His Creation, particularly on humankind.

A 2006 newspaper poll in the US found that 61% of American Christians agree with the idea that God wants people to be prosperous. I believe that God does want some people to prosper financially, but not for the purpose of lining their own pockets so that the money is just spilling out. There is enough wealth in the world to allow all eight billion of us to live in comfort, with full bellies and roofs over our heads. Some super-wealthy people have recognised their duty to share, and freely give money to assist the needy or to attempt to eradicate disease. Since floating the idea of persuading rich people to give at least 50% of their wealth to charity in 2009, the 'Giving Pledge' that was founded by Bill Gates and Warren Buffett has raised hundreds of billions of dollars from several hundred US billionaires. But they are the exception – and of course they've given from their excesses. After all, how many billions of dollars does a person need to live on?

The televangelist Kenneth Copeland has a personal reported net worth of up to 760 million US dollars. Perhaps God will say to Copeland when he turns up at the Pearly Gates: *"What did you do with all the money I lent you? Did you use it to feed My people? What! You used it to buy mansions, private jets and expensive cars?"* But Copeland is not the only televangelist who has misinterpreted Jeremiah 29:11. Others with obscene levels of personal wealth include Pat Robertson, Joel Osteen, Benny Hinn, Creflo Dollar (now there's a suitable name!), Rick Warren, Franklin Graham (son of the late, great Billy Graham), TD Jakes and Joyce Meyer.

We are called by God to live for His Kingdom, not ours.

Pastor Nicholas McDonald wrote an article in January 2015 titled, **Why the Prosperity Gospel Is the Worst Pyramid Scheme Ever**. When he was in college, McDonald was taken in by a prosperity gospel preacher, causing him to embrace that movement. He said, *"I was bamboozled by the prosperity pastor's ploy in the same way people are fooled by pyramid schemes. They see the success of the guy at the top, and think: It's working for him, isn't it?"*.

In **Gospel Transformation Notes**[23], about Mark 12:38-44, the author says:

> In sharp contrast to his proud and exploiting opponents, 'who devour widows' houses' (verse 40), Jesus praises the sacrificial devotion of a poor

---

[23] © 2013 by Crossway

widow. Her singular trust in God serves as a powerful example and as a penetrating window into God's opinion of true greatness and significance. The widow's devotion exposes the exploiting self-interest of those officials who handle temple taxes and tithes. Her devotion also indicates complete dependence on God. She gives all that she has, expecting him to provide all that she needs. Her willingness to put God's honour above all other priorities applies to us all, even as we carry out our biblical responsibilities to provide for the welfare of our families and communities.

Others

I get angry when Christian pastors misquote the Bible, often for their own selfish ends. In February 2021, during a complete lockdown of Melbourne city, the pastor of The Revival Christian Church in the suburb of Narre Warren, Paul Furlong, defied the Government by holding a church service. Furlong was interviewed on the national news, saying, *"God commands in the Bible not to forsake the gathering of the people to gather for church, and I obey the commands of God, not man".* Furlong misquoted the Bible, which actually says, *"And let us consider how we may spur one another on toward love and good deeds, not giving up meeting together, but encouraging one another…"* (Hebrews 10:24-25).

Furlong would have done well to read Romans 13:1, which says, *"Let everyone be subject to the governing authorities, for there is no authority except that which God has established. The authorities that exist have been established by God".*

The Forest and the Trees

The Bible is God's *love story* to us. It is a story of love, justice, grace and forgiveness.

But the Church has a tendency to take hold of a particular verse or passage and use that as a rod with which to beat people it disagrees with. Not only does it not consider that it may have misinterpreted the words God spoke – as I explain below – but it takes them out of context and is clearly selective about which passages it wants to make an issue of. For example, one of the commands given by God is: *"Do not eat any meat with the blood still in it"*

(Leviticus 19:26). Of course the Church won't insist that we follow that one, or its leaders wouldn't be able to eat a juicy steak!

The issue is not with specific verses in the Bible, but with its overall message. Let us not get so hung up on analysing the trees that we miss seeing the forest in all its beauty. In other words, focusing on a particular verse or passage can cause us to miss the overall message.

Misinterpretation of the Bible

Let's return to the concept of anamorphic art that I introduced in the Prologue. In the modern interpretation below of Tommaso Laureti's concept, you can look at the lump of clay from every angle; but one perspective, and one perspective only, will reveal the image of a frog. That perspective happens in this case to be a reflective cylinder.

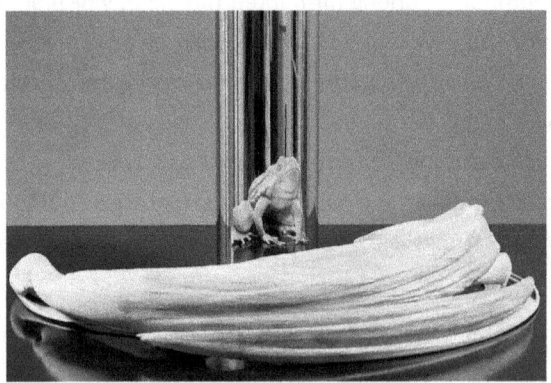

Similarly, you can look at the Bible from every angle, but one perspective – and one perspective only – will reveal its true meaning. <u>That perspective is the cross.</u>

Christians have misinterpreted the Bible ever since Jesus was here on Earth. Even now, many Christians believe that 'God hates fags' – as the late Fred Phelps, pastor of Westboro Baptist Church in the US, infamously maintained. But I believe that they're wrong: God loves everyone.

Many Pentecostal churches seem to have been particularly good at misinterpreting verses about tithing, for their own financial advantage.

"'Bring the whole tithe into the storehouse, that there may be food in My house. Test Me in this,' says the Lord Almighty, 'and see if I will not throw open the floodgates of Heaven and pour out so much blessing that there will not be room enough to store it'" (Malachi 3:10).

Sadly, many churches have turned church into a 'business', cajoling their congregations into giving huge amounts to the church, on the grounds that God would bless their socks off if they were really generous with their tithes and offerings. As I said earlier in this chapter, one of the few times that we see Jesus getting really angry is when He was in the courts of the Jerusalem temple in the lead-up to Passover:

"In the temple courts He found people selling cattle, sheep and doves, and others sitting at tables exchanging money. So He made a whip out of cords, and drove all from the temple courts, both sheep and cattle; He scattered the coins of the money changers and overturned their tables. To those who sold doves He said, 'Get these out of here! Stop turning My Father's house into a market!'" (John 2:14-16).

Just as the Jerusalem temple had become a place of business, too many of today's Churches seem to have forgotten that God meant for it to be somewhere that people would come to meet with Him and to worship and praise Him.

I sometimes wonder about the motivation for the preachers who focus on prophesying and casting out demons. Some of them may not even be Christians. I remember attending a *Full Gospel Business Men's Fellowship* dinner in Sydney, where an American preacher called up anyone who suffered from back pain. In every instance, he told them it was because they had one leg longer than the other, and he then prayed the legs into the same length. Of course it was only the euphoria of the moment that caused those 'healed' to rejoice in the miracle this man had brought upon them, and the ones I spoke to subsequently realised that they had been conned. Jesus called out these 'false disciples': *"Not everyone who says to Me, 'Lord, Lord,' will enter the Kingdom of Heaven, but only the one who does the will of My Father who is in Heaven. Many will say to Me on that day, 'Lord, Lord, did we not prophesy in Your name and in Your name drive out demons and in Your name perform many miracles?' Then I will tell them plainly, 'I never knew you. Away from*

Me, you evildoers!'" (Matthew 7:21-23). I hasten to add that miracles do happen, but I doubt that everyone in that meeting with chronic back pain suffered from unequally-long legs!

One of the world's most famous astronomers, Galileo, was put under house arrest in 1632 by Pope Urban VIII after he had presented evidence to support his theory that the Earth revolved around the sun. He was never released, dying ten years after his arrest. It wasn't until 1822 that the Roman Catholic Church acknowledged that Galileo had been right, although it would be another 170 years before Pope John Paul II – following a 13-year investigation into the Church's condemnation of Galileo – officially acknowledged its error of 360 years earlier. (I wondered how the investigation could have taken 13 years, until I remembered that it took them 190 years to even acknowledge what everyone else in the world knew about astronomy well before 1822). Galileo had been forced to recant his scientific findings as 'abjured, cursed and detested', in order to avoid being burned at the stake. (Incidentally, Copernicus had initially developed this theory of *heliocentrism* in 1543.)

The Pharisees, Sadducees and teachers of the law in Jesus' day knew their Bible inside out, but failed to interpret it properly, resulting in their murdering of Jesus, God's only Son. The whole of the Old Testament provided clues to the coming of the Messiah, and Isaiah 53 in particular should have made it abundantly clear to the Jews that Jesus was, in fact, the long-awaited Saviour of their people.

The Bible was used to justify slavery until 1833 in England and 1865 in America. It was used in Germany to condemn six million Jews to death in World War II. It was used to justify discrimination against coloured people in the US, until Rosa Parks' refusal to give up her seat on a bus to a white man in 1955 finally brought some sense to the people – although it wasn't until 1967 that the US Constitution finally allowed interracial marriage, after Richard and Mildred Loving had fought to have their 1958 marriage recognised nationally. It was used to discriminate against women, and to justify their subjugation to men. And it is being used even now to discriminate against gay people. How Satan must love the church hierarchy! He doesn't need to attack gays – the Church is doing that for him.

Harper Lee's classic historical novel, **To Kill a Mockingbird** is a horrific account of racial discrimination in America in the 1930s. I found myself seething with anger when a clearly innocent man was convicted of raping a white girl, simply because he was black. The local Negro community's church pastor said something that was actually true of life back then: *"I ain't ever seen any jury decide in favour of a coloured man over a white man"*. Chatting with God about that afterwards, I told Him that I was still angry – even though this particular incident was fictional. I said how it must grieve Him to see the extent of man's inhumanity to man. After all, it was God who chose the colour of our skin, not us. But God reminded me that it has not been so different for gay people. From the 1970s through to the 1990s, the police in Sydney have estimated that 27 Sydney men were murdered, simply because they were gay. Most of those men were thrown off cliffs at spots frequented by gays, such as those just north of Sydney's iconic Bondi Beach. How could people justify that? After all, it was God who chose the 'colour' of our sexuality, not us.

If the Church is so adamant that only heterosexual marriage is acceptable, why does it not also condemn people who have been divorced? There are many people in just about every church who have not only been divorced, but have now remarried. If the church won't recognise gay marriages, how can it accept people who deliberately ignore Jesus' teaching on adultery?

And as for celibacy within the Roman Catholic Church priesthood, where did that come from? Certainly not from the Bible. Paul, who said he would prefer it if people remained single, like him, said, *"But if they cannot control themselves, they should marry, for it is better to marry than to burn with passion"* (1 Corinthians 7:9). It's no wonder that the Roman Catholic Church is in danger of destroying itself as a result of its failure to recognise that its own priests would be very unusual if they did not 'burn with passion'.

As I have tried to convey in these pages, the Bible has been misinterpreted for many centuries, and probably ever since it was written – particularly the Old Testament. Undue emphasis is given to the commands in the Old Testament, many of which ceased to have effect once the New Covenant came into being. For example, the Old Testament commanded that unblemished newborn lambs be sacrificed regularly for the sins of the people. We don't do that today. We don't need to. A lot of church leaders seem to be unaware that there is a New Covenant, and that the rules of the Old Testament no longer apply. Jesus brought this New Covenant into being with His death on the Cross. The era of sacrificing animals as an atonement for sin, for example, was then over. Jesus became the perfect sacrifice for us.

The word 'homosexual' was first used in the Bible when the Revised Standard Version (RSV) was published in 1946. Ed Oxford, a gay Christian and theological college graduate, has done a lot of research into this topic for his upcoming book, co-written with Kathy Baldock, **Forging a Sacred Weapon: How the Bible Became Anti-Gay**. Ed discovered that Martin Luther translated the original Greek word *arsenokoitai* not as 'homosexual', but as 'molester of boys'. It wasn't until 1983 that German Bibles started to replace the term 'boy molesters' with 'homosexuals', and that was only due to pressure from their publishers. (Coincidentally, it was the Germans who first coined the word 'homosexual', in 1862.) I recommend that you get a copy of Ed's book when it is published, as he has made some astonishing observations regarding our misinterpretation of the Bible. I cover this practice of adult males having sex with pre-pubescent boys a bit later.

****

So what did Jesus actually talk about in His three short years of ministry? I have identified six topics that I believe are most relevant for us: Love, grace, forgiveness, holiness, compassion and salvation, which I will cover in detail in the next chapter.

Rob Buckingham is a respected Senior Minister at Melbourne's **Bayside Church**. Rob wrote in **Thoughts on Same-Sex Marriage** in 2015: *"The Christian message is not predominately a message of morality; it is a message of redemption. Now redemption should lead to morality but I think we sometimes get the cart before the horse. We build walls instead of bridges and keep people out of the kingdom because of our 'moral' stand just like the Pharisees did. Read Matthew chapter 23 and see how unimpressed Jesus was with this kind of attitude"*.

God's demands should not be confused with those of His delegates, though, as they are not always right. The well-known evangelist, Joyce Meyer, is a real Old Testament follower. She believes that anyone who deliberately disobeys any of the Law will go to Hell, and has condemned gay people in this way. I explained earlier the fallacy of such thinking. I believe Meyer was also misguided on the meaning of tithing in her sermon titled **God Is Faithful and True (Part 2)**. Malachi 3:10 says this: *"Bring the whole tithe into the storehouse, that there may be food in My house"*. If we want to apply the principle to our lives today, I believe that it is to be taken literally. In other words, we are to give for the purpose of feeding people in physical need of food. Meyer said that the food referred to is the Word of God, not real food, and that its purpose is to feed the people spiritually. She also insisted that the 'storehouse' is the church. She did not say that this was only her interpretation of that verse, but that it was an incontrovertible fact that God was referring to spiritual 'food'. But Malachi 3:10 was actually a command given to the Old Testament Israelites to provide for the nutritional needs of the priests, whose occupations precluded them from being able to do so themselves.

Joyce Meyer said also that her congregation could not even use any of their tithe to help the poor, and that any such giving had to be in addition to the ten per cent they give to her church. *"You can't buy my tapes with part of your tithe, either"*, she maintained. But what really annoys me was her assertion that, if we don't tithe in the way she stipulated, God won't protect us from car accidents and the like! Joseph Prince had a good response to people like Meyer in a devotional based on Isaiah 53:4-5:

> One of the most evil teachings that I have heard is that God will chastise His own with sicknesses, diseases, accidents and tragedies. Do you know that this erroneous teaching is actually based on the old covenant and not the new covenant? In Leviticus 26:28, God says to those who fail to obey His commandments, 'I will chastise you seven times for your sins.' But guess what? You are no longer under the covenant of law. You are under the covenant of grace! Jesus has already borne all your chastisement and punishment on the cross. Read it for yourself in today's Scripture, then reread it and reread it once more.
>
> The prophet Isaiah saw a prophetic vision of our Lord Jesus on the cross, bearing the punishment for our transgressions. He declared that the chastisement that we deserved came upon Jesus so that you and I will never have to go through what He endured on our behalf. And by the stripes laid on Him as He bore our chastisement, we are healed! Hallelujah!
>
> So how can anyone have the audacity to say that God will still chastise us with sicknesses, diseases and accidents today? To say this is to negate the

finished work of Jesus Christ! Under the new covenant, God will never again chastise the believer for his sins!

Like many other televangelists, Meyer has become very wealthy on the back of her ministry. She (of course!) has a private jet and several million-dollar homes.

****

Jesus had a lot to say about morality and right living, so what did He say about homosexuality? Absolutely nothing! That's right: A topic that sucks all the energy from many churches these days was apparently not considered significant enough by Jesus for Him to even mention it.

That's not to say that the Bible is completely silent on the matter. But, as is the case with most Bible injunctions, the comments regarding male-to-male sex need to be taken within the context of the people who were being addressed.

At first glance, the following verse seems pretty damning of homosexual behaviour: *"If a man has sexual relations with a man as one does with a woman, both of them have done what is detestable. They are to be put to death; their blood will be on their own heads"* (Leviticus 20:13).

But what about the following verses from the same chapter of Leviticus?

"A man or woman who is a medium or spiritist among you must be put to death. You are to stone them; their blood will be on their own heads" (Leviticus 20:27).

"Anyone who curses their father or mother is to be put to death. Because they have cursed their father or mother, their blood will be on their own head" (Leviticus 20:9).

"If a man commits adultery with another man's wife – with the wife of his neighbour – both the adulterer and the adulteress are to be put to death" (Leviticus 20:10).

Just in case you're feeling a little self-righteous at this point, let me remind you of a few more commands from Leviticus and Exodus:

"Do not eat any meat with the blood still in it. Do not practise divination or seek omens. Do not cut the hair at the sides of your head or clip off the edges of your beard. Do not cut your bodies for the dead or put tattoo marks on yourselves ... Do not degrade your daughter by making her a prostitute, or

the land will turn to prostitution and be filled with wickedness. Observe My Sabbaths and have reverence for My sanctuary... Do not turn to mediums or seek out spiritists, for you will be defiled by them ... Stand up in the presence of the aged, show respect for the elderly and revere your God. I am the Lord" (Leviticus 19:26-32).

"Keep My decrees. Do not mate different kinds of animals. Do not plant your field with two kinds of seed. Do not wear clothing woven of two kinds of material" (Leviticus 19:19).

"For six days work is to be done, but the seventh day is a day of Sabbath rest, holy to the Lord. Whoever does any work on the Sabbath day is to be put to death" (Exodus 31:15).

Oops! I'm sure at least some of that lot caught you out.

Thankfully, the Old Covenant became irrelevant when Jesus came to bring a New Order.

It's clear that the story of the city of Sodom (from which we have erroneously coined the term sodomy) is not about homosexuality. It is much more likely, as Rev. Samuel Kader says in his excellent book, **Openly Gay, Openly Christian**, that the people gathered outside Lot's house were more of a 'lynch mob', ready to do a *Ku Klux Klan* ritual on the men who were staying with him. The Hebrew word for what the people of Sodom wanted to do to Lot's guests (who were not actually men, but angels) has been misinterpreted. They said that they wanted, not to 'know' the guests in a sexual sense, but to *yada* them. That word means to 'know deeply' and, while it can be used to describe sexual intimacy, it is also used to describe how God knows us and how we can know Him. There was a word in Hebrew that they could have used if they had really wanted to imply that sex would be involved.

Of course, even this interpretation could be wrong. But think about it for a minute. Let's say that the entire male population of the city of Sodom wanted to gang-rape the two visitors (no small feat in itself!). Using that interpretation, we have to conclude that Lot was offering his two virgin daughters, both of whom were engaged to be married, to be gang-raped! Presumably, this sick scenario would also involve the two fiancés. Do you seriously believe that God would condone such an act, while condemning male-to-male sex? What sort of a God would consider that to be right?

Yet people in the Church continue to use the fate of Sodom to justify their belief that 'God hates fags'. God explained later that the reason He destroyed Sodom was that its inhabitants were selfish and self-centred. It probably had nothing to do with homosexuality.

"Now this was the sin of your sister Sodom: She and her daughters were arrogant, overfed and unconcerned; they did not help the poor and needy. They were haughty and did detestable things before me. Therefore I did away with them as you have seen" (Ezekiel 16:49-50).

No sane person today would believe that the entire male population of Sodom was gay, as the wording of the story in Genesis would appear to suggest. In any case, the raping of a man by another man in Old Testament times was simply a means of proving who was boss. It had nothing to do with homosexuality as we know it today. Abraham pleaded with God to spare Sodom, to which God finally agreed – if Abraham could produce as few as ten righteous people from the entire population (and, by 'righteous', He didn't mean that they were heterosexual). Of course he couldn't, just as there isn't a city in the world today that could produce even one righteous person.

Paul also appears to refer to homosexual behaviour as an 'abomination' in one of his New Testament letters[24]. But, once again, this needs to be seen in context. At that time, it was common for men to engage in sex with prepubescent boys – a practice that even today most people consider unacceptable. This was what Paul was so strongly opposed to.

Fundamentalist Christians assert that God made us to be heterosexual, and some even say that marriage is for the purpose of procreation . I presume that also means that God does not make anyone asexual. But here's an interesting statement by Jesus Himself:

"For there are eunuchs who were born that way, and there are eunuchs who have been made eunuchs by others – and there are those who choose to live like eunuchs for the sake of the Kingdom of Heaven. The one who can accept this should accept it" (Matthew 19:12).

There was an article in Sydney's **The Daily Telegraph** on 18 June 2015 titled **Bizarre Catholic Marriage Warning**. The Roman Catholic Church had just

---

[24] Romans 1:18-32

distributed a booklet to schools, asserting that allowing gay marriage would open the way to marriages between 'throuples' (a *ménage à trois*), in addition to all manner of other relationships. This was a bit rich, coming from people whose church won't allow them to marry and who have turned a blind eye to paedophilia within their own ranks for decades – and perhaps centuries.

Finally, after much prayer, soul-searching and studying of the Bible, I came to the conclusion that, for one reason or another, God had allowed me to be gay. More importantly, it was liberating to at last realise that God had accepted me for who I was, and that I, too, could accept my sexuality as being God's will for me.

Of Wine and Wineskins

Joseph Prince, in **Destined to Reign**[25], wrote:

> The devil has also succeeded in erecting fences around the gift of righteousness. Today, conventional theology teaches you that not only is there such a thing as 'positional righteousness', there is also something known as 'practical righteousness'. They are saying that even though you were made righteous by grace, you now have to do right and keep the law to continue being righteous. They call this having 'practical righteousness'.

Why is attendance at mainstream churches declining so rapidly? Could it be that the churches have lost their first love, The Lord Jesus Christ? The Bible is God's love story to us. We need to concentrate on its core message. It is a story of love, grace, forgiveness and holiness. It is not about fostering hatred and bitterness towards groups in our society who may be different from us. Just as Christians for the last 2,000 years have used the Bible to justify slavery, as well as discrimination against women and coloured people, they're repeating the same mistakes in respect of their gay brothers and sisters. The world would be a better place if everyone realised that the only thing that really matters in life is having a personal relationship with Jesus.

Satan has succeeded in getting the Church to focus on issues that have nothing to do with salvation. You have only to read the plethora of material

---

[25] © 2011, Joseph Prince

from pastors and church leaders about God's alleged hatred of homosexuality to realise that the Church has a one-track mind – and it's on the *wrong* track! How can it not see that its focus is so misplaced? How can Christians come to realise that God is concerned with *whose* we are, and not at all with *who* we are? They are so obsessed with the perceived sin of gay people that they have forgotten to preach the Good News!

Old and new wineskins

As I said in Chapter 1, I am absolutely astounded that, after 2,000 years, the Christian church still does not understand what Jesus was talking about when He said, *"No one sews a patch of unshrunk cloth on an old garment. Otherwise, the new piece will pull away from the old, making the tear worse"* (Mark 2:21). As if the point needed reinforcing, which in hindsight it certainly did, He gave another analogy: *"And no one pours new wine into old wineskins. Otherwise, the wine will burst the skins, and both the wine and the wineskins will be ruined. No, they pour new wine into new wineskins"* (Mark 2:22). Why do churches persist in their belief that Christians are free from some of the Law, but not all of it?

I read an article titled, **America's Microwave Christianity – The Heart of the Present-Day Church Must Change**, by Shane Idleman. I certainly agree that 'the heart of the present-day church must change', but I do not agree with Idleman in how he believes it should change. He said, *"Do you ever wonder how a Christian (let alone a pastor) can embrace gay marriage and encourage it?"* Why does he not promote the message of salvation through Jesus Christ alone, rather than carrying on about peripheral issues that have nothing to do with people's souls?

Paul reminded the Christians in Galatia that they no longer had to follow Jewish practices, as set out in the Law. He warned them against trying to earn God's favour by their behaviour, as well as cautioning them against using the Law to judge people who did not belong to their community. Charles Stanley said: *"The temptation to be legalistic was strong back then, and it's just as strong 2,000 years later"*.

"It is for freedom that Christ has set us free. Stand firm, then, and do not let yourselves be burdened again by a yoke of slavery" (Galatians 5:1).

"You who are trying to be justified by the law have been alienated from Christ; you have fallen away from grace" (Galatians 5:4).

An author wrote in **Gospel Transformation Notes**[26] on Hebrews 1:3 about this tendency for Christians to pour new wine into old wineskins:

"Christians sometimes do not act as if Christ's sacrifice were finished, perfect and effective. When they sin, they sometimes beat themselves up spiritually and do a form of evangelical 'penance', as if their extra prayers, promises and tears can somehow atone for their sins. It is right to be displeased with ourselves when we sin. But there is no other antidote to the poison of sin than Christ's sacrifice. We dishonour Him and His death if we act otherwise".

Joseph Prince said much the same thing in his devotional of 14 December 2020, titled **Nothing Means Nothing!**:

> I often hear people say, 'God's love is unconditional!' But the moment they fail, all of a sudden, the love they once said was unconditional becomes contingent upon their behaviour. Many believe that God loves them when they do right, but stops loving them the moment they do something wrong. Well, I'm going to shatter that wrong belief into smithereens with the truth of God's Word!
>
> While our love for God can fluctuate, His love for us always remains constant. His love for us is based on who He is and not based on what we do [my emphasis]. I love just how confident and emphatic the apostle Paul is when he says, *'For I am persuaded that neither death nor life, nor angels nor principalities nor powers, nor things present nor things to come, nor height nor depth, nor any other created thing, shall be able to separate us from the love of God which is in Christ Jesus our Lord'* (Romans 8:38-39). In the New International Version, it says, *'For I am convinced…'*.

The Samaritans

Most of us know the parable that Jesus told of the Good Samaritan, who went out of his way to help the victim of a vicious robbery on the road from Jerusalem to Jericho. But there's a lot more relevance to us today regarding

---

[26] © 2013 by Crossway

the Samaritans than just that story, which I discovered while doing research for this book.

Firstly, the Samaritans practised something called *syncretism*, which is *'the amalgamation or attempted amalgamation of different religions, cultures or schools of thought'* (**Lexico Dictionary**). In their case, it was the mixing of a belief in foreign idols with that of Jehovah (God). How stupid was that? But that is basically what today's Church is guilty of as well. It tries to blend the concept of salvation by grace with works.

My second observation concerned the treatment by the Jews of the Samaritans, which reminded me of how gays are treated today by the Church. Samaria was a region between the north and south kingdoms of Israel. The Samaritans were considered by the Jews to be unclean, having interbred with the Assyrians, who had conquered them long before Jesus appeared on the scene. Jews went out of their way to avoid meeting Samaritans. The most devout ones would even cross to the east bank of the Jordan River when heading north or south between the two Israeli kingdoms, and then cross back again once they had cleared Samaria. I believe that gay people in our day can identify with the Samaritans. We're considered unclean by the Christian Church, which goes out of its way to avoid us.

What about Other Religions?

I do not consider Christianity to be a *religion* as such, so it can't be grouped with the religions I am about to refer to. As Josh McDowell said in **More than a Carpenter**[27], *"Religion is humans trying to work their way to God through good works. Christianity is God coming to men and women through Jesus Christ offering them a relationship with Himself"*.

Another statement I read recently summed it up nicely: *"Religion kills and keeps people in bondage, but Christ brings life and freedom"*.

I don't profess to understand everything about what the Bible means when it says that salvation is only obtainable through Jesus. What about people in darkest Africa who have never heard of Him? The only contribution I

---

[27] © 1977 by Josh McDowell

can make to this discussion is that I believe we are all born with a sense of who God is, and also that we will be judged on the knowledge that was available to us at the time. But I certainly don't believe that people who have rejected the truth about Jesus, for whatever reason, will actually see Heaven.

All religions require their adherents to work their way to Heaven. Christianity is the only belief system whose God came down to Earth knowing that no one could ever be good enough to get to Heaven by their own efforts.

I was shocked to learn in August 2019 that 52 per cent of American Protestant Christians believe salvation comes from faith plus works, as if Jesus' sacrifice on the cross were not enough to pay the penalty for our sins. These people, along with the 1.3 billion Roman Catholics worldwide, are practising a form of religion. Whether they have truly experienced God's forgiveness is not something to be debated here. But the fact is that they are missing out on God's abundant blessings for them if they are constantly in fear that He will strip them of their salvation if they set a foot wrong. And, let's face it, we all sin daily.

This verse, uttered by John, is probably the best-known verse in the Bible:

"For God so loved the world that he gave his one and only Son, that whoever believes in him shall not perish but have eternal life" (John 3:16).

John goes on in the next two verses to reinforce the above truth.

"For God did not send his Son into the world to condemn the world, but to save the world through him. Whoever believes in him is not condemned, but whoever does not believe stands condemned already because they have not believed in the name of God's one and only Son" (John 3:17-18).

When Australia's State of Victoria outlawed gay conversion therapy in 2019, the Managing Director of the **Australian Christian Lobby**, Martyn Iles, said *"You're actually criminalising a significant part of the Christian faith. That's hugely concerning for the Christian community ... I think there are things that need to be stopped, but if we're getting into this kind of conversation – steady on. It's just attacking religion."* As I say frequently throughout this book, attacking religion is a good thing!

When Thomas asked Jesus how he and his fellow disciples could know the way to Heaven, Jesus answered, *"I am the way and the truth and the life. No one comes to the Father except through Me"* (John 14:6).

After Jesus' death, His disciple Peter said: *"Salvation is found in no one else, for there is no other name under Heaven given to mankind by which we must be saved"* (Acts 4:12).

Most religions rely on good behaviour to get their adherents to Heaven. They seem to believe that if you've been more-good-than-bad, you will have earned your ticket. Christianity is the only belief system where God came to man, because He knew that no one could pass the stringent entrance exam into Heaven, with 100 per cent being the 'pass' mark. *"Be perfect, therefore, as your Father in Heaven is perfect"* (Matthew 5:48).

It is distressing for me to know that many of the people I love are marching headlong towards Hell. Most people want to believe that it doesn't exist, which is playing right into Satan's hands. Their argument is that a loving God would not condemn any of His precious children to eternal punishment. But He does not condemn anyone – they condemn themselves. God sacrificed His own dear Son to enable us to avoid that fate. God doesn't send anyone to Hell; we are already on our way there!

Judaism

Old Testament prophecies

There are apparently 351 Old Testament prophecies that were fulfilled in Jesus. As I have said in 0, the odds of only eight of them having been fulfilled in one man are astronomical.

Yet the Jews are still waiting for the Messiah to come, more than 2,000 years after He made His very dramatic entrance into, and even more dramatic exit from, our world.

All Israel will be saved

Israel declared independence in May 1948, having until then been regarded as Palestinian territory. The Jews believed God had ordained that they would lay claim to certain disputed territories within and around Israel. In April/May 1967, Egypt's President Nasser tried to cripple tiny Israel by banning Israeli shipping from the Straits of Tiran, as well as ordering his forces to advance into the Sinai Peninsula, where they expelled a **United Nations** peacekeeping force that had been guarding Israel's border for over a decade.

Faced with such threats, in June that year Israel launched pre-emptive air strikes against Egypt and its allies, crippling the Egyptian air force. It then staged a ground offensive, seizing the Sinai Peninsula and the Gaza Strip from Egypt, the West Bank and East Jerusalem from Jordan, and the Golan Heights from Syria. This war, which significantly altered the geopolitical landscape of the Middle East, was over in six days! While 10,000 Arabs were killed, only 800 Israelis died.

Since then, Israel has been engaged in a number of wars with its Arab neighbours, none of which it lost.

What is so remarkable about these conflicts is that Israel is a tiny nation compared to its aggressors. For example, Egypt alone had a population of 32 million in 1967, while Israel's was 2.7 million.

How could such a tiny country be victorious against an enemy so much bigger than it? In exactly the same way that the small youth, David, overcame the giant Goliath. David and Israel both had God behind them.

Ezekiel 38-39 predicts a great final war to be waged between Israel and a number of other countries. This is yet to happen, but in 2022 I believe it is imminent. While the names quoted in those chapters do not correspond with the current names of the countries that will attack Israel, it is believed that the main aggressor, Magog, is modern-day Russia. (Gog is the leader of Magog). Persia is, of course, Iran. Cush appears to be Sudan and Ethiopia. Put is probably Libya. Togarmah is possibly Anatolia, which comprised most of modern-day Turkiye[28]. Gomer could be Turkiye or Germany. I suspect it's Turkiye, whose president, Recep Erdogan, cosied up to Russia's Vladimir Putin in September 2021 to discuss strategic alliances. Things are hotting up!

"The word of the LORD came to me: 'Son of man, set your face against Gog, of the land of Magog, the chief prince of Meshek and Tubal; prophesy against him and say: "This is what the Sovereign LORD says: I am against you, Gog, chief prince of Meshek and Tubal. I will turn you around, put hooks in your jaws and bring you out with your whole army—your horses, your horsemen fully armed, and a great horde with large and small shields, all of them brandishing their swords. Persia, Cush and Put will be with them, all with

---

[28] Turkiye is, itself, a new name, having been known as Turkey until 2022.

shields and helmets, also Gomer with all its troops, and Beth Togarmah from the far north with all its troops—the many nations with you"'" (Ezekiel 38:1-6).

The Jewish people have been blessed and favoured by God ever since the time of the Exodus, more than 3,000 years ago. I believe that God will continue to protect Israel right through to the end. I have long prayed that the whole world will recognise God's hand, when He supernaturally defends Israel against the attack by Russia and its diabolical allies. Romans 11:26 says that *"all Israel will be saved"*. I don't understand why Israel is the 'Promised Land', especially since the Jewish people don't believe that the Messiah has even come yet, but there is no doubt that it is a nation favoured by God.

Roman Catholicism

The Roman Catholic Church is wrong about homosexuality. But, even worse, it has completely misunderstood the message of salvation. While doing research for this book, I read much of the Catholic Church's 1,425-page **Catechism**. It is basically 1,425 pages of rules its adherents must follow if they want to gain and retain their salvation.

Many of its beliefs are mind-boggling. For example, an infant who dies before it can be baptised won't go to Heaven. And since even the Catholics agree that there is no place other than Heaven or Hell after Jesus returns in judgement, then it follows that babies go to Hell if they die before they can be baptised. What needless anguish these beliefs must bring to the parents.

If you have sinned since your last confession, and you die in the meantime, you will be put into a holding cell (called *Purgatory*) until you are *purged* of your sins. And you had better hope that your family and friends are praying for you while you're in Purgatory, to reduce the time you have to spend there. Purgatory is never mentioned in the Bible. It was introduced in one of the Apocrypha (books that were written between 200 BC and 400 AD).[29] [30]

---

[29] From the Apocryphal book: 2 Maccabees (chapter 12; verses 39-46)

[30] I've included a number of the Catechism 'rules' in the Appendix, together with references to its item numbers.

Why does the Roman Catholic Church classify itself as Christian? With 73 books in their bible, the Roman Catholic Church does not even believe in the Bible that is recognised by Christian churches.

The Catholic Church makes a big thing of making our lives right before we can worship God. But I am already right with God – permanently! This idea of having to confess my sins regularly – and the Catholic Church seems to think that weekly is sufficient – is something that the Church has conjured up.

Nowhere in the Roman Catholic Church's Catechism does it say that it is a sin to be gay. In fact, the Church has acknowledged that people do not choose to be born with a particular sexual orientation. According to the Catechism, however, homosexual practice is 'intrinsically disordered' and 'contrary to natural law'. It says that 'homosexual persons are called to chastity'.

The Catholic Church's Catechism says that gays and lesbians can and should approach 'Christian perfection' through chastity. It has missed the whole point of Jesus' coming to Earth. Christians are perfect from the moment they accept Jesus as Lord. Perfection is not something they have to strive for.

The **New York Times** carried an article about homosexuality in the Roman Catholic Church in its 17 February 2019 edition. This is some of what the writer, Elizabeth Dias, said:

> The stories of gay priests are unspoken, veiled from the outside world, known only to one another, if they are known at all.

> Fewer than about ten priests in the United States have dared to come out publicly. But gay men probably make up at least 30 to 40 percent of the American Catholic clergy, according to dozens of estimates from gay priests themselves and researchers. Some priests say the number is closer to 75 percent. One priest in Wisconsin said he assumed every priest was gay unless he knows for a fact he is not. A priest in Florida put it this way: 'A third are gay, a third are straight and a third don't know what the hell they are.'

In 2019, French journalist Frédéric Martel published a 570-page book titled **In the Closet of the Vatican**. In this book, he claimed that 80 per cent of priests working in the Vatican are gay, although not necessarily sexually active. He said that, from his observations, some of the most publicly homophobic senior clerics in the Vatican are themselves gay.

On 19 May 2002 the then-Catholic Archbishop of Sydney, the Most Reverend George Pell, refused Holy Communion to gay and lesbian parishioners, telling the congregation at St Mary's Cathedral that *"God made Adam and Eve, not Adam and Steve"*, and saying that *"important consequences follow from this"*.

The **Sydney Morning Herald** reported on the following day: *"Dr Pell's rejection of about 20 parishioners marked the first time members of the Rainbow Sash movement had sought communion from the archbishop since he moved to Sydney a year ago. As archbishop of Melbourne, he refused Sash members communion at least 10 times"*.

In May 2019 I found myself yelling abuse at the television set, because of a comment on a fictional thriller! It was the second instalment of Agatha Christie's **ABC Murders** that raised my ire. The hero, Hercule Poirot, was standing in the middle of his Roman Catholic church, talking with his parish priest, when he confessed to some sins. The priest told him that he had to repeat his confession in the confessional at the front of the church in order for God to absolve him – that God wanted to forgive him, but he had to confess his sins in the orthodox Catholic way. What angered me about this representation was that this is what really happens in the Catholic Church. Its adherents seem to think of God as some cosmic schoolmaster, determined to enforce the rules and to wield the cane at anyone who dares to step out of line. I wonder what happens to a Catholic who, when confessing their sins to the priest, has forgotten one of them. Are they then not cleansed?

Here's another statement from the Roman Catholic Church's **Catechism**:

> The church teaches that, as one does not choose to be either homo- or heterosexual, being gay is not inherently sinful. According to the Catholic theology of sexuality, <u>all sexual acts must be open to procreation</u> [my emphasis] and express the symbolism of male-female complementarity. Sexual acts between two members of the same gender cannot meet these standards. Homosexuality thus constitutes a tendency towards this sin but also can make an individual less culpable for it.
>
> The Church teaches that gay people are called to practise chastity. They also teach that gay people 'must be accepted with respect, compassion and sensitivity,' and that 'every sign of unjust discrimination in their regard should be avoided.'

I found the comment *'homosexuality thus constitutes a tendency towards this sin but also can make an individual less culpable for it'* absolutely extraordinary. Is the Church saying that God will overlook sins, depending on who committed them?

It is interesting that the former (Anglican) Australian politician, the Reverend Fred Nile, used to embrace the Catholic Church's position on marriage being for the purpose of procreation until, when his wife Elaine died, he married someone else. By that time Nile was 79 and his new wife, Silvana Nero, 55, so I doubt that he married her for the purpose of procreation. Earlier, Nile had said about marriage: *"The Bible says it's between a man and a woman for the means of procreation"*. Nile has always made himself out to be a man of principle, but his actions in marrying Ms Nero call this reputation into question. His change of standard in this simply reinforces my observations that we believe what we want to believe, and that we will revise our beliefs if they no longer suit our own agenda.

The Catholic belief that its adherents are being continually forgiven when they go to Mass and confess their sins is intrinsically flawed. They simply haven't grasped the fact that, at salvation, Christians are forgiven <u>once and for all</u>. The writer to the Hebrews said this of Jesus' sacrifice: *"Unlike the other high priests, He does not need to offer sacrifices day after day, first for His own sins, and then for the sins of the people. He sacrificed for their sins once for all when He offered Himself"* (Hebrews 7:27).

The Catholic Church used to have a rule that forbade even starting the process of canonisation of someone until five years after their death. Following pressure from Mother Teresa's followers soon after her death in 1997, Pope John Paul II agreed two years later to waive that rule, and to immediately begin the process of making her a saint. And, of course, in the Catholic Church the Pope is the only one who can actually confer sainthood upon a person. It usually takes two approved/documented miracles for someone to be considered for sainthood, though martyrs only need to have performed one. What a distortion of Biblical principles!

Sydney's **The Daily Telegraph** carried an article in October 2020 about a 15-year-old Italian boy, Carlo Acutis, who had died in 2006. Describing the boy as a 'blessed millennial', Pope Francis spoke of his beatification by the

Catholic Church the day before. The Vatican claims that Acutis interceded from Heaven in 2013 to cure a Brazilian boy who was suffering from a rare pancreatic disease. How the Church could even suggest that Acutis performed a miracle from Heaven is an example of just how weird this religion is. Once he performs a second miracle from Heaven, Acutis will officially be declared a saint.

But all Christians are saints. Writing to the Romans, Paul said, *"He gave me the priestly duty of proclaiming the gospel of God, so that the Gentiles might become an offering acceptable to God, sanctified by the Holy Spirit"* (Romans 15:16). The word 'sanctified' comes from the Latin *sanctus*, meaning *holy*, as does the word *saint*.

****

In 2018, the Holy See entered into a compact with the Chinese Government, regarding the appointment of bishops in China. It was renewed in 2020. Is it any wonder that Satan was happy for this to happen? He has nothing to fear from the Catholics regarding people turning to Jesus. In fact, because Roman Catholicism gives people a false sense of security, it is actually in Satan's interest to promote it in China. I think the Chinese authorities even understood this!

Why won't the Anglican Church call out the Catholics? It's because they are birds of a feather, particularly the Catholics and the 'high' Anglican church.

Why won't the Pentecostals call out the Catholics? I believe the Pentecostal Church is worried that if they were to do that, the Catholics would call *them* out on their own flawed thinking – particularly regarding the Prosperity Doctrine.

Why won't the Uniting Church call out the Catholics? For the most part, I believe that the Uniting Church does not actually know what the Gospel is about. They don't actually understand why Roman Catholicism is not Christian.

****

I can still remember a dream I had as a small boy. A house was on fire but, because its driveway was too steep for the fire engine to get to it, the brigade decided to extinguish the blaze at a house on the other side of the street. But that house was not on fire. Can you see the analogy between that dream and the Christian churches of today? The Church, having decided that the fire of the Catholic Church presents too much of a challenge, has trained its hoses on the house of homosexuality. But that house is not on fire.

Christian Churches

Before I get stuck into the Church for its erroneous beliefs, I need to point out that no matter how many theological degrees a church leader may have, it is the Holy Spirit who imparts wisdom and insight in Bible interpretation to us. Writing to the Corinthians, Paul attested to this fact as well. *"My message and my preaching were not with wise and persuasive words, but with a demonstration of the Spirit's power, so that your faith might not rest on human wisdom, but on God's power"* (1 Corinthians 2:4-5).

I value my commitment to simply know God as far more important than any theological training. My Old Testament hero, David, had been a mere shepherd boy, not a highly educated theologian. He did some despicable things, such as committing adultery and then murder. Yet he was described by God as *"a man after My own heart"* (Acts 13:22). Why was that? I believe it was because he longed to know God, spending his life in this pursuit.

In **Our Daily Bread** on 30 October 2018, Mart DeHaan gave a clear warning to the Church about how it applies its beliefs:

> The way to agree to disagree is to recall that each of us will answer to the Lord not only for our opinions but also for how we treat one another in our differences. Conditions of conflict can actually become occasions to remember that there are some things more important than our own ideas – even more than our interpretation of the Bible. All of us will answer for whether we have loved one another, and even our enemies, as Christ loved us.

A number of my dear friends rejected me when I told them I was gay. I don't really blame them, as that is exactly how I believe many Christians would react. But the Church in general is culpable, with clergy who should at least understand the Scriptures fuelling the hatred of gays by their congregations. It just staggers me that Christians, who of all people should know that we are all imperfect, could actually believe that God hates any of the people that He has created.

We can get caught up in the minutiae of the Bible. But what is important for all of us to realise is that it is God's Love Story to us. From Genesis to Revelation, it is about love, grace, forgiveness and holiness. Satan uses people to discredit the Bible, even those who have been appointed to serve God in the pulpit.

Churches generally believe that homosexual practice is wrong, and most believe even that it is wrong to *be* homosexual – as if we gay people had any say in the matter. Even if they do accept that we are born gay, they demand celibacy from us. I believe that some Christians are called to a celibate life, regardless of their sexual orientation, but what about non-Christians? If between five and ten per cent of the population are gay, that's an awful lot of people to be condemning.[31] Or is gay sex wrong only for gay Christians?

****

Let us now look at the beliefs and practices of the established Christian churches. I can only speak here of Australia's mainstream churches, although I suspect their counterparts in other countries are not very different.

Anglican Church

The Anglican Church is wrong about homosexuality.

Some Anglican schools in New South Wales wrote an open letter to Members of the Federal Parliament in October 2018 objecting to proposed changes to the anti-discrimination laws. They wanted to be able to refuse employment to gay people, and even to sack any of their employees whom they subsequently found were gay.

I wrote the following letter about this, and sent it to the influential media outlet, **News Ltd**.

---

[31] It seems that, as more and more people in society feel comfortable about their sexuality, the percentage of gay people as reported in surveys continues to increase. The Australian Human Rights Commission reported in 2019 that up to 11 per cent of Australians 'may have a diverse sexual orientation, sex or gender identity'.

The hypocrisy of the Anglican Church, as well as its school leaders, is breathtaking. I refer to the article quoted in **The Australian** last week, which said that the principals of some of Australia's leading Anglican schools argued that the exemptions in the Sex Discrimination Act are *'the only significant legal protections available to schools to maintain their ethos and values with regard to core issues of faith'*. What is so outrageous about this, though, is that Anglican schools in some Australian dioceses have no such concerns when it comes to employing staff and teachers who are not even Christians. Speaking to **The Australian**, Dr John Collier, the head of school at St Andrew's Cathedral School in Sydney, said he signed the letter to reinforce the views of religious schools. *'It is a significant moment when my fellow school heads feel strongly enough to write an open letter to MPs'*, Dr Collier told **The Australian**. *'Our joint concerns go to the heart of school ethos and missions.'* What *missions* was Dr Collier referring to? If he means that the Anglican Church has a mission to teach the truth of salvation only through Jesus Christ, then why do many Anglican schools engage to serve in the 'front lines' teachers who don't even believe in that mission? And what makes a gay Christian unable to fulfil that mission? Thankfully, Glenn Davies, the then Anglican Archbishop of Sydney, quickly issued a rebuttal of the letter from the school principals, saying that Anglican schools would never discriminate against gay people, whether they are students or prospective (or existing) staff.

Watching the **Netflix** series, **The Crown**, incensed me. The Archbishop of Canterbury, who lived (and the present Archbishop still does) in the magnificent Lambeth Palace, was all about pomp and ceremony. God was not directing him when he told Queen Elizabeth II that her coronation had to be 'traditional'. He also told David Windsor (formerly King Edward, who abdicated to marry the American, Wallis Simpson, a divorcée) that his wife would not be permitted to attend the coronation. How could this man have risen to hold the highest office, other than the Queen, in the Church of England? What sort of example does that set for non-Christians?

Uniting Church in Australia

The Uniting Church is wrong about homosexuality.

To be fair, it has now given its individual churches the right to perform same-sex marriages, while also allowing for those congregations that are strongly opposed to homosexuality in general – and same-sex marriage in particular – to stay true to *their* beliefs.

The Uniting Church has also completely misunderstood the meaning of the word *baptism*, as used by Jesus. It has become a rule for salvation, as evidenced by this extract from its **Basis of Union**:

> <u>The Uniting Church acknowledges that Christ incorporates people into his body by Baptism</u> [my emphasis]. In this way Christ enables them to participate in his own baptism, which was accomplished once on behalf of all in his death and burial, and which was made available to all when, risen and ascended, he poured out the Holy Spirit at Pentecost. Baptism into Christ's body initiates people into Christ's life and mission in the world, so that they are united in one fellowship of love, service, suffering and joy, in one family of the Father of all in heaven and earth, and in the power of the one Spirit. <u>The Uniting Church will baptise those who confess the Christian faith, and children who are presented for baptism and for whose instruction and nourishment in the faith the Church takes responsibility</u> [my emphasis].

When we get baptised in water, we are simply celebrating the fact that we belong to Jesus and that He lives in and through us. But the baptism that Jesus spoke about was symbolic, in that it meant we were immersed in Him. *"So in Christ Jesus you are all children of God through faith, for all of you who were baptised into Christ have clothed yourselves with Christ"* (Galatians 3:26-27).

Baptist Church

The Baptist Church is wrong about homosexuality.

As with most mainstream denominations, there is a diversity of opinion within the Baptist Church, so I do not want to condemn those churches that do accept homosexual relationships. However, the **Southern Baptist Convention** in the United States, the largest Baptist group in the world (with 15 million members), says some pretty inflammatory things about homosexuality. It refers to homosexuality as a 'lifestyle', saying it is a 'manifestation of a depraved nature', 'a perversion of divine standards' and 'a violation of nature and natural affections'. It also describes it as 'an abomination in the eyes of God'.

Interestingly, the **Southern Baptist Convention** came into being because the Christians who lived in the south disagreed strongly with the push by the north to abolish slavery, which eventually resulted in the American Civil War.

The southern Baptists argued that the Bible condoned slavery. It suited them to have slaves, as the cotton farms that were so prevalent in the south were heavily labour-dependent. This is another example of what I said earlier: We will believe what we want to believe.

But the Baptist Church – and I'm speaking here in general – has a lot of ideas that are incompatible with Jesus' teachings. For example, they believe it is wrong to drink alcohol, forgetting that Jesus' first recorded miracle was to produce wine from water at a party – where many people were probably already drunk! And Paul told Timothy that he should drink 'a little wine' to help with his sickly condition. Incidentally, I found it interesting that some of the principals of Baptist schools, while outwardly condemning the consumption of alcohol, would happily imbibe in the privacy of dinners we shared. Some also do not approve of dancing, although it seems more likely that they are just party-poopers than that they are following any command in the Bible.

Pentecostal Church

The Pentecostal Church is wrong about homosexuality.

I served as bursar at a well-known Pentecostal Christian school in Sydney for six years, and I have no doubt that, had I come out as gay during my tenure there, my services would have been terminated. As it was, I was at that time hiding my sexuality not only from my employers, but also from myself.

I have attended a number of Pentecostal churches over the years. As a rule, they are filled with people, both clergy and laity, who truly love the Lord. But I have generally found them to be anti-gay. Once again, these churches have missed the whole point of the New Covenant. They try to combine the gift of grace that Jesus brought, at horrendous personal sacrifice, with Old Testament rules. Jesus never turned away anyone because of who they were.

United Church of God

This church is just plain wacky.

It says, *"There is simply no excuse for believing that Jesus came to abolish any commandments of God"*[32]. Did they forget that God issued 613 commandments in the Old Testament, or do they believe that we have to obey the other 603 as well? It goes on: *"But, to our shame, the Ten Commandments have been rejected as the standard of human behaviour by our society. Even many who profess to follow Christ today treat them as irrelevant because they have been taught that God's law was abolished at Christ's death"*.

Sadly, this church has missed the whole point of the Ten Commandments. As I have said, God gave the commandments to His people, not with the expectation that they would follow them, but to show that it was *impossible* to follow them. When a member of the United Church of God tries to explain to God at the entrance to the Pearly Gates that they had tried to obey the Ten Commandments, I can imagine God saying, "So you don't think My Son's sacrifice was enough? You thought you needed to give Him some help?"

Reformed Church

The Reformed Church has some diabolical beliefs.

I wonder where the Holy Spirit fits into their thinking? There is clearly no room for a DPR with Jesus in their beliefs, as they assert that He can't talk to us outside His Word.[33] Its adherents clearly miss out on so much of what God has for us. This is what they say:

Reformed theologians believe that God communicates knowledge of himself to people through the Word of God. People are not able to know anything about God except through this self-revelation. Speculation about anything which God has not revealed through his Word is not warranted. The knowledge people have of God is different from that which they have of anything else because God is infinite, and finite people are incapable of comprehending an infinite being. While the knowledge revealed by God to people is never incorrect, it is also never comprehensive.

---

[32] United Church of God – **Beyond Today: The Ten Commandments in the New Testament**, 14 February 2011

[33] Of course, any DPR with Jesus must accord with the Word of God.

Why the Church Is Wrong

The Christian Church is just as broken and sinful as it makes the gay community out to be. When Reverend Jide Macaulay, about whom I talk later in this chapter, tried to approach the bishops in his own Church of England denomination in England, he was not even granted an audience. Is the Church so scared to hear the other side of the argument, lest it become tainted? Is it so broken and sinful that it does not even want to look at how it can be repaired? It seems to me that it is afraid to face head-on the difficult questions that need to be asked of it. Ironically, this is exactly what Martin Luther faced in 1517 with the Catholic Church, when he sent his **95 Theses** to his Archbishop as a prelude to debating his then-radical beliefs. That debate never took place.

In his amazing book, **Twisted Scripture**[34], Andrew Farley attacks religious tradition, saying that, like Jesus, we need to stand up to churches that are caught up in this. *"What does this mean for us? <u>We can expect to go **outside** the walls of religious tradition to find the truth about Jesus and to honour all that He has done for us</u>* [my emphasis]. *Some don't like the smell of real freedom. They prefer bondage and would like to drag us inside the city walls and into a temple of religiosity where we too can be fixated on effort and works instead of Jesus"*.

Farley hit the nail on the head: Churches are so bound by the Old Testament laws that they have imprisoned their followers, instead of proclaiming to them the incredible joy of being free in Christ.

I have read so many books giving both sides of the argument as to what the Bible really says about homosexuality that it has made my head spin. My conclusion regarding this debate is that, as with most things that have strong arguments both for and against a position, we will believe what we want to believe. I gave two glaring examples of this earlier in this chapter.

It is important to note here, though, that regardless of what the Church thinks about homosexuality, it has always existed and that is not going to change. What is different now is that society, in general, no longer views it as

---

[34] © 2019 by Andrew Farley

a sickness, and many people do strive to treat gay people as no different from anyone else.

But what we believe about homosexuality is not the point. The Church has no right to disenfranchise someone simply because they don't fit into their mould. Jesus accepted people just as they were. He dined with hated tax collectors and sinners, and even associated with prostitutes. The point, surely, is that it is the Church's mandate to lead *everyone* to Jesus. And then, when someone has invited Jesus into their heart, they have actually ceased to be a sinner in the eyes of God – but only because of Jesus' finished work on the cross.

As I said earlier, God sees me as perfect. I am still gay. You are still selfish, or self-centred, or divorced, or ... <u>If you are a Christian, God doesn't see your sin. He sees you only through the blood of Jesus, His precious Son.</u> What God does with that person after they've been saved is between them and God, no one else.

As I mentioned earlier in this chapter, Mildred Jeter (a woman of colour) and Richard Loving (a white male) met during the 1950s, fell in love and were married in Washington DC in 1958. When they returned to their home in Virginia they were arrested and faced spending a year in prison unless they left the state. Eventually, they challenged the Virginia law and in 1967 it led to a landmark Supreme Court decision, in which Chief Justice Earl Warren said, *"Marriage is one of the basic civil rights of man, fundamental to our very existence and survival"*.

Christian singer/songwriter Trey Pearson, who came out as gay at the age of 35, said, *"The handful of Bible verses that directly address homosexuality do not prohibit the kind of loving, committed gay relationships known to the modern world. There is absolutely no conflict with accepting who I am and following Jesus ... God wants me to be healthy, authentic, whole, integrated and my truest self"*.

So why does the Church not proclaim the truth here? For a start, I believe that the people who make the most noise are those with the most to hide. I was reminded of the saying, *Methinks he doth protest too much*[35]. I can speak

---

[35] From Shakespeare's **Hamlet**: *"The lady doth protest too much, methinks"*.

from experience here. I used to denounce gays quite vehemently, proudly telling others that I was praying for rain during Mardi Gras (Sydney's Gay Pride festival) and denouncing their adoption of the word *gay* – which used to mean *happy* or *colourful*. I was one of those who made the most noise!

Christians have been made right by faith in Jesus, not by obeying Old Testament law, as Paul clearly pointed out: *"Before the coming of this faith, we were held in custody under the law, locked up until the faith that was to come would be revealed. So the law was our guardian until Christ came that we might be justified by faith. Now that this faith has come, we are no longer under a guardian"* Galatians 3:23-25).

Selective interpretation

The Church likes to be selective in its application of the laws in the Bible. It condemns homosexuality but, as I have already mentioned, what about the other laws that are listed in the Old Testament, such as in Exodus 31:15? *"For six days work is to be done, but the seventh day is a day of sabbath rest, holy to the Lord. Whoever does any work on the Sabbath day is to be put to death"*. Sorry, pastors, but you have to be put to death.

The outspoken Christian author, Beth Moore, came in for a barrage of criticism in 2019 for her failure to condemn gay marriage. A few months later, in October of that year, the influential pastor John MacArthur spoke about Beth's support of women in ministry: *"Go home!"*, he said. Was this guy really representing Jesus? His vile attack on Beth Moore would suggest not. MacArthur said, *"There is no case that can be made biblically for a woman preacher – period, paragraph, end of discussion"*. Of course his words, 'end of discussion', show that he has a closed mind. I suspect MacArthur was afraid that women really are serving Jesus in ministry, so he attacked all women preachers with this comment: *"They want power, not equality"*. What a narrow-minded, bigoted individual he is. Incidentally, at the time of writing, MacArthur was reported to have a net worth of 14 million US dollars, so of course he would not want to share the pulpit with a whole new cohort of pastors who might be the recipients of tithes that would otherwise have found their way into his coffers.

MacArthur's prejudice is no doubt based on these verses, which I quoted in my Prologue:

"Wives, submit to your own husbands as you do to the Lord. For the husband is the head of the wife as Christ is the head of the church, His body, of which He is the Saviour. Now as the church submits to Christ, so also <u>wives should submit to their husbands in everything</u> [my emphasis]" (Ephesians 5:22-24).

Don't you find it odd that the Church can take the verses about homosexual sex literally, while failing to do so with verses such as the one above?

Living in sin

I would like to address these next words to homophobic Christians.

Do you always obey the laws of the land? How about exceeding the speed limit while you're driving? Parking illegally? Taking a pen home from your workplace? Claiming expenses you are not entitled to on your tax return? If you were able to say 'no' truthfully to all of those questions, and other similar ones, that's great. But here's the clincher: Do you *"Love the Lord your God with all your heart and with all your soul and with all your mind"*? (Matthew 22:37). I suspect that every one of us will have to answer 'no' to that one. If that's the case for you, <u>you are living in sin</u>. So I suggest you take the plank out of your own eye before you try to remove the speck from the eye of your gay brother or sister.

It seems that every day I am bombarded with online articles by Christians condemning homosexuality, if not homosexuals. Most of them say that a gay lifestyle – or even not actively renouncing one's homosexual orientation – is anathema to God. Their reasoning is that God won't tolerate deliberate sin. But every one of us sins deliberately every day. We are all living in sin.

The Bible tells us to repent of our sin, so most Christians will tell us that if the Holy Spirit abides within us, we cannot continue to sin. Admittedly, all but the completely delusional must admit that there may be chronic periods of transgression, but they say that the Holy Spirit works in us to change our desires and practices. As I have said, I believe that Christians don't sin *wilfully*. But we do sin *deliberately*– every day. I think theologians have misinterpreted what John was saying in one of his letters about sin. *"No one who lives in Him keeps on sinning. No one who continues to sin has either seen Him or known Him"* (1 John 3:6). I interpret that verse to mean that people who really are Christians are no longer *seen* by God as sinners.

Even if we are to believe the Church's interpretation of 1 John 3:6, there is a difference between deliberate sin (which every one of us is guilty of every day) and wilful sin (which I don't believe a Christian would ever be guilty of).

Whenever we choose our own way over God's way we are living in sin. And isn't that the case for all of us most of the time? Paul said that *"everything that does not come from faith is sin"* (Romans 14:23). I think that's a pretty clear message to us that we are all living in sin!

The point I want to make is that God does not care about our sexuality. All that matters to Him is that we have a DPR with Him. Why can't so many in the Christian community understand that?

Many churches welcome gay people, correctly following Jesus' example of welcoming everyone. But, sadly, most of them do so in the hope of convicting them of their 'sin', thereby getting them to renounce their homosexual lifestyle – if not their homosexuality.

Failure to accept a whole subset of society

To the churches that reject gay people I would say this: Every human being is loved by God. The early Christians, including Peter, believed that certain people were – by birth – loved by God, while others were rejected by Him. It was only after Peter received a vision from God, together with the admonition to not treat anything He had created as unclean, that he realised we are all equal in God's eyes.

"Then Peter began to speak: 'I now realise how true it is that God does not show favouritism but accepts from every nation the one who fears him and does what is right'" (Acts 10:34-35).

But returning to Joyce Meyer. As one of the more famous evangelists in the United States, she has an enormous following, particularly among women. But she is wrong when she talks of God's judgement. She has said that she can't allow gay people to stay in her church unless they renounce their homosexuality. She has also said, incidentally, that she would terminate the employment of any member of her staff who was in a relationship that was not under a marriage covenant. Once a person becomes saved, God Himself does not condemn them. So why should she?

As with the Church in general, how many gay people have had the door to salvation slammed in their face at Meyer's church? The brother of a friend of mine grew up in the Anglican Church, serving as a youth leader as an adult. But when he came out as gay he was kicked out of the church. He was even disowned by his father. This happened at least twenty years ago, and he hasn't returned. That church has a lot to answer for.

We are a fallen people, and have been ever since Adam and Eve disobeyed God and ate the forbidden fruit. There isn't a 'righteous' person in the whole world. What we all need to remember, though, is that anything we do during our fleeting time on this Earth that is not of God is insignificant. On Judgement Day we will face either eternal punishment or eternal joy. Which it will be is our decision, but Christ's ambassadors in this broken world have a responsibility to introduce everyone we possibly can to our King.

Alan Turing, whose mathematical genius played a pivotal role in the Allies' victory in World War II, was gay. Despite acknowledgement by the British Government that his work had probably shortened the war by two years and saved over 14 million lives, it was his homosexuality that took prominence. Given the option of imprisonment or chemical castration, Turing chose the latter. Queen Elizabeth II granted him a posthumous pardon in 2013, and he was honoured in 2019 when he was depicted on the Bank of England's new £50 note. But it was too late to help Turing. He died tragically at the age of 41 from cyanide poisoning. History is full of examples of how misguided the Church has been over the ages.

The same thing happened with women 2,000 years ago.

Romans treated women as nothing more than baby-producing machines, having no other real value. And Roman fathers had the absolute right to decide if their newborn baby would live or die. If it had birth defects, and often even if it was merely a girl, the father could turn his head away, indicating that the child had to be taken out to the woods or the local garbage tip to die. But Jesus valued women and showed it. How shocking this must have been to the Romans at that time! The Church is metaphorically doing the same thing today to gays.

In October 2019, the then-Anglican Archbishop of Sydney, the Rev. Dr Glenn Davies, made an outrageous statement in his presidential address to the Sydney Anglican Diocese Synod, specifically to same-sex marriage proponents in the Anglican Church. He said that such people should *"start a new church or join a church more aligned to their views – but do not ruin the Anglican Church by abandoning the plain teaching of scripture"*. What an absolutely un-Christian pronouncement. In any case, the Anglican Church has already been ruined, because it has *'[abandoned] the plain teaching of scripture'*.

Where's Jesus?

Love, grace and forgiveness are what we should be concentrating on. My wife of 23 years asked me how I could have married her, knowing I was gay. I told her (having believed the lies of the church) that I had believed God would cure me of my same-sex feelings, especially through marriage. I did not actually believe that I was gay, unaware that it was innate. How many people's lives have to be hurt in this way? It's not only the gay person who suffers under this dogma.

I think it is important to stress some very pertinent Scriptures: What does Leviticus say about homosexuality? What does it say about adultery? Eating shellfish? Wearing two types of cloth? What did Paul say about homosexuality? What did he say about women speaking in church? About women being submissive to their husbands? What did Jesus say about homosexuality? What did He say about divorce? You can read about most of these issues in Leviticus 11 and 18-20, 1 Corinthians 14 and 1 Timothy 2. But you will not find in the Bible what Jesus said about homosexuality, because He was completely silent on the subject. Why was He silent on an issue that has paralysed the Church today? It's not as if it did not exist back in Biblical times. Perhaps Jesus just didn't think homosexuality was much of an issue. Perhaps He didn't think it was an issue at all.

Jesus had heaps to say about adultery, however. He said that marriage is meant to be for life. How many Christians do you know who have divorced? My thought is that we have changed over the centuries, but not for good. We are now outside God's original plan for us, but the fact is that we *have* changed. What was unacceptable then is now acceptable, in a strange sort of way. In any case, as I said earlier, those issues have nothing to do with salvation.

I am in a unique position. Having been a Christian for forty-five years, I can't imagine not being one. But I have also known almost all my life that I am different, and that, similarly, there is no chance that I am able to give up my homosexuality. In that way I am a bridge between two shores, much as Jesus was a bridge between Heaven (since He was truly God) and Earth (as He was also fully human).

<u>There is absolutely nothing more important in life than knowing Jesus Christ as our Lord.</u> Everything else will fall away, but our relationship with Him will last forever. Do we build a wall or a bridge?

Joe Stowell wrote in **Our Daily Bread** on 22 October 2018: *"If hurting, rejected people can find loving refuge, comfort and forgiveness in Jesus, they should expect no less from the church. So let's exhibit the love of Jesus to everyone we encounter – especially those who are not like us. All around us are people Jesus wants to love through us".*

Martin Luther King said, *"God is not interested merely in the freedom of black men, and brown men, and yellow men; God is interested in the freedom of the whole human race".* He then said, *"I have decided to stick with love. Hate is too great a burden to bear".*

God had planned my existence long before I was born. Do you think He didn't know I would be gay? Would He suddenly reject me when I turned to homosexuality? God knew before I was born that I would be sinful and alienated from Him and unable to change– that I needed a Saviour. I will always be a child of God. *"For those who are led by the Spirit of God are the children of God"* (Romans 8:14).

I believe that the Church in general is obsessed with sex. It has even distorted the Word of God to further its own ends. The story of Sodom, which I have referred to earlier, is one such example. But how often do pastors preach about the *deliberate* sin that almost everyone on Earth commits on an ongoing basis: The failure to love God above all others, and to have no other gods but Him?

The following article by Rachel-Claire Cockrell was published in an issue of **Crosswalk** on 10 February 2020:

> I know that Paul tells the churches to expel sinners from their midst. He encourages us not to indulge someone in sinful behaviour. We use those verses to justify judgement of others and I believe this is a gross misinterpretation of scripture. Yes, we are to hold each other accountable, but I would never deign to call out a stranger or even an acquaintance on some perceived sin. I will hold my husband accountable, as he does for me. I know he loves me, so when he gently rebukes an action of mine I know that he is only encouraging me to better myself, just as I do the same for him. That is what Paul is talking about when he says to hold fellow brothers and sisters accountable in love. He is not talking about condemning others. <u>Every time a Christian judges someone based on skin colour, sexual orientation, gender, socioeconomic status, promiscuity (the list goes on, you get the idea), then they are acknowledging the belief that they are better than that person. The truth of Jesus is in our equality. We are all sinners in need of a Saviour. Christians have accepted Christ and avoided condemnation based on faith and the grace of God. We do not avoid condemnation based on our own actions. Every time we think less of someone else, we forget that we are also sinners</u> [my emphasis]. Paul himself claimed that he was the 'worst of all sinners'. If Paul considers himself the worst sinner – a man who dedicated his life to spreading the gospel of Christ and who wrote most of the New Testament – how much more of a sinner am I? The only way to avoid this sin is to acknowledge our own weaknesses and to embrace humility. In fact, that could help us avoid a multitude of sins.

Churches need to consider what Jesus was saying: *"And if you greet only your own people, what are you doing more than others? Do not even pagans do that?"* (Matthew 5:47).

The last book in the Bible, **Revelation**, was written as a prophecy by one of Jesus' disciples, John, to the seven churches in Asia Minor. I have always found the third chapter to be particularly scary, as it refers to so many of our so-called Christian churches today. God gave John the following words:

"I know your deeds, that you are neither cold nor hot. I wish you were either one or the other. So, because you are lukewarm – neither hot nor cold – I am about to spit you out of my mouth. You say, 'I am rich; I have acquired

wealth and do not need a thing'. But you do not realise that you are wretched, pitiful, poor, blind and naked" (Revelation 3:15-17).

Dr Robert Schuller's Crystal Cathedral, home to the weekly televised church service in Los Angeles, **Hour of Power**, was such a church. The largest glass building in the world, and housing the fifth-largest pipe organ in the world, it was certainly very opulent. On the one occasion that I attended a service there, it felt to me that they had everything in that church – except Jesus![36]

Satan doesn't need to set up his own churches, although I understand there are official satanic churches in existence. Christian churches are doing his job for him.

Why People Don't Attend Church

The number of people in the world who describe themselves as Christian is in a steady decline. A 2018-19 survey in the U.S. by the Pew Research Center found that 65 per cent of American adults now describe themselves as Christian, down from 77 per cent in 2009. There were an estimated 329 million people in the US in 2019, including 74 million who were under eighteen years old, which means that about 30 million adults have ceased to identify as Christian in ten years in the US alone! Over 66 million adults in the U.S. claim to have no religion at all.

I did some research among my non-church-going friends and family to determine why people don't go to church these days. There was a common thread to their thinking:

1. Churches seem fixated on Jesus (I wish they were!), ranking Him ahead of their own families. In every case where this has been a concern, the family has been the respondents' most important reality.
2. Christians seem to be narrow-minded and arrogant, denigrating other religions and asserting that Jesus is the only way to Heaven. (I

---

[36] Incidentally, the church filed for bankruptcy in 2010, owing over 43 million US dollars, and the beautiful building that had purportedly been built 'to the glory of God' is now owned by the Roman Catholic Church.

wish they *were* narrow-minded, because Jesus *is* the only way to Heaven!)
3. Gay people believe (because they are told so) that they are not welcome in the majority of churches or that, if they are, they will be urged to become straight.
4. Christians seem to care less than people in other sectors of society about helping people in physical need. They don't seem to realise that you need to show people you care about their physical needs – the ones that dominate their thoughts all day every day – before you have earned the right to lead them to Jesus.

What the Church Must Do

Above all, love each other deeply.
1 Peter 4:8

Agree on what is important

The Church and the gay community are not going to agree in the near future.

A group of Moravian Christians, who lived in 1722 in what is now the Czech Republic, found they were arguing all the time on Christian perspectives. But then they decided to focus on what they agreed upon, rather than on what divided them. The result was unity. As that Moravian community discovered, we are set free and brought into unity through Jesus. Whatever our culture, status, gender or sexuality, we are all one with Christ. Our identity, future and spiritual freedom are found in Him alone.

With all the discord today regarding homosexuality and the Church, couldn't we all follow the example of those Moravians? There is so much to agree upon! Paul says in Ephesians 4:3, *"Make every effort to keep the unity of the Spirit through the bond of peace"*. So why do churches have to sow discord, thereby alienating the whole gay community?

A dear friend of mine, who attends an Anglican Church, often says to me when I speak about my beliefs (such as on the topic of salvation only through

Jesus), *"We'll have to agree to disagree"*. With most arguments, that is probably the approach I should follow as well, but I can't just stand by when the topic is, literally, of life or death. It was apparently John Wesley who coined that phrase in the 18th century, when he gave a tribute to his long-time friend and sparring partner, George Whitefield, upon the latter's death. Wesley said: *"There are many doctrines of a less essential nature… In these, we may think and let think; we may 'agree to disagree'. But, meantime, let us hold fast the essentials"*.

I am frequently criticised for being dogmatic. Christians who state definitively that salvation is found only through Jesus are frowned upon by a society that has come to believe, in respect of religion, that anything goes. As I once read in a devotional, *"Christian dogma is grounded in the love of Christ, who died out of love for all people on the cross"*.

A sign was posted at the front of the Walnut Grove Baptist Church in Dallas, North Carolina in March 2017, saying:

"Just love everyone. I'll sort 'em out later. God."

Dave Branon wrote in **Our Daily Bread** on 27 April 2017: *"Before you tell others about Christ, let them see how much you care"*.

Whether this is true or not doesn't matter, as John's letters speak for themselves, but I heard a tale of a conversation between *"the disciple Jesus loved"*, John, and one of John's own disciples. John's disciple complained to him that all of his letters (which we now know as 1 John, 2 John and 3 John) talked of nothing but love. *"Can't you talk about something else?"*, he asked. *"There isn't anything else"*, John replied. What a sad indictment of our church today that our leaders have failed in their God-given mission to *love* people into the Kingdom.

A story I remember from my childhood concerned a debate between the sun and the wind as to which of them was stronger. It was actually one of Æsop's fables, titled **The North Wind and the Sun**:

> The North Wind boasted of great strength. The Sun argued that there was great power in gentleness.
>
> "We shall have a contest," said the Sun.

Far below, a man travelled a winding road. He was wearing a warm winter coat.

"As a test of strength," said the Sun, "Let us see which of us can take the coat off of that man."

"It will be quite simple for me to force him to remove his coat," bragged the Wind.

The Wind blew so hard, the birds clung to the trees. The world was filled with dust and leaves. But the harder the wind blew down the road, the tighter the shivering man clung to his coat.

Then, the Sun came out from behind a cloud. Sun warmed the air and the frosty ground. The man on the road unbuttoned his coat.

The sun grew slowly brighter and brighter.

Soon the man felt so hot, he took off his coat and sat down in a shady spot.

"How did you do that?" said the Wind.

"It was easy," said the Sun, "I lit the day. Through gentleness I got my way."

The sun sent so much warmth down to the man that he took the coat off himself.

Are you going to try to push people into accepting that what you believe is right, or are you going to send warmth to all people, so that they will want to come in of their own accord?

I believe that the Church, while correctly pointing out that Christians have been forgiven, fails to understand that they have also *been made righteous*. It seems to me that if I sin, the Church is telling me that I have lost my holiness, if not my forgiveness.

****

Reverend Jide Macaulay is a British-Nigerian, who was born in London but spent his teenage years in Nigeria, where he had his first homosexual experience. His father, Professor Augustus Macaulay, is the president of Nigeria's **Association of Christian Theologians**, of which Jide is a member. He was the founder of Nigeria's second-largest university, **United Bible University**, where he was also Director of Studies. When Augustus learned that his son was gay, he wrote to Jide, saying that his homosexuality was *"not only ABOMINABLE* *but a great DISGRACE to our family"*. He said he would be happy if Jide were to be imprisoned for fourteen years under Nigeria's strict anti-gay laws – which in the Muslim north even stretch to punishment of death by stoning. Augustus actually seemed to believe that prison might turn Jide straight!

As an ordained clergyman in the Church of England, Jide has been told that it is OK that he's gay, but it is not OK for him to marry his partner, nor to engage in gay sex, on pain of excommunication. The Archbishop of Canterbury not only refused to meet with Jide, but also refused to allow him to meet with any of the bishops of the Anglican Church. How can church leaders refuse to even engage people in conversation on the topic of homosexuality? Are they worried that their beliefs might change or, worse, that they might become gay themselves? I find it incredible that people whose vocation is to be ambassadors for Christ refuse to even engage with people whom they deem to be sinners. But what is more amazing for me is the fact, as I have stated elsewhere in this book, that around fifty per cent of ordained clergy in the Church of England are not even Christians!

Jide made a very profound statement at the conclusion of the 2019 BBC documentary, **Too Gay for God?**: *"I know I am not too gay for God, but perhaps I am too gay for this religious institution"*. Sadly, the Church of England – and, indeed, the Anglican Church worldwide – is now simply an 'institution', rather than what the Bible refers to as a 'church'.

Follow Jesus' example

The woman caught in adultery

As noted earlier, John Chapter 8 tells of a woman caught in the act of adultery, for which the penalty was death by stoning. When the Pharisees and their partners-in-crime, the 'teachers of the law', tried to trap Jesus into breaking their law by forgiving her, Jesus simply said to them, *"Let any one of you who is without sin be the first to throw a stone at her"* (John 8:7). That got them! After they had all walked away in shame, Jesus asked the woman, *"Woman, where are they? Has no one condemned you?"* (John 8:10). When she replied that no one had condemned her, Jesus said, *"Then neither do I condemn you ... Go now and leave your life of sin"* (John 8:11).

Notice that Jesus did not order her to promise to leave her life of sin before He forgave her. That was afterwards. She was already forgiven.

Zacchaeus

Zacchaeus was a hated tax collector. He was appointed by Rome to collect taxes from the people and, like most people who had that authority in Jesus' day, he added a good measure for himself. Of all the people in Jericho at that time, Zacchaeus was probably the most hated. Imagine him on the day Jesus came to Jericho. A small man, he had to climb a sycamore tree to be able to see Jesus.

Did Jesus also condemn Zacchaeus for his cruel treatment of his fellow Jews? Let's see what happened:

"When Jesus reached the spot, He looked up and said to him, 'Zacchaeus, come down immediately. I must stay at your house today'" (Luke 19:5).

That was all Zacchaeus needed to repent of his evil practices. In response to this, Jesus declared to the people around Him: *"Today salvation has come to this house"* (Luke 19:9). Jesus welcomed Zacchaeus *before* he had repented. Incidentally, I found it interesting that Jesus said to Zaccheus, *"I must stay at your house today"* [my emphasis]. Was Jesus giving us a message that we, too, must spend time with social rejects? Does He want us all to welcome into our churches people whom *we* may perceive as unacceptable to God?

Welcome everyone!

The Christian Church today has an amazing opportunity to make things right. Homosexuality is right out in the open now, and no one can be in any doubt that it is here to stay. Just as in the above examples, churches should welcome gay people publicly, opening their doors to the multitude of men and women who have until now been denied the opportunity of even hearing about Jesus in their establishments.

David Bennett writes in **A War of Loves**[37] about the failure of Christians to follow Jesus' example: *"Some of us have sinfully failed to reach out to, value and love the gay community but are very happy to moralise and judge. This is far removed from the radical holiness and truth, on one side, and compassion*

---

[37] © 2018 by David Bennett

and mercy, on the other, that Jesus showed to 'outsiders'. His example leads the way for us".

CHAPTER 4

The Bible

And this gospel of the kingdom will be preached in the whole world as a testimony to all nations, and then the end will come.
Matthew 24:14

What Does the Bible REALLY Say?

The saying 'Love is what makes the world go round' is absolutely spot-on. Moses was given the Ten Commandments on Mt Sinai but, as Jesus pointed out centuries later, these two are the key to the whole of life:

"Jesus replied: 'Love the Lord your God with all your heart and with all your soul and with all your mind.' This is the first and greatest commandment. And the second is like it: 'Love your neighbour as yourself.' All the Law and the Prophets hang on these two commandments" (Matthew 22:37-40).

Why do people get hung up on all the other laws, especially those that applied under the *Old Covenant*? Why do some of my former Christian friends condemn me for eating shellfish?[38] Oh, that's right: They've chosen to ignore that one; it's just the *gay* thing that concerns them.

---

[38] Leviticus 11:9-10

Here is another verse that shows what God is about today: *"And now these three remain: Faith, hope and love. But the greatest of these is love"* (1 Corinthians 13:13).

God is love. He doesn't love just some people, some of the time. He loves everyone, all the time. He wants us to love others in the way He loves us. He does not want us to take offence when people upset us – He wants us to love them.

Paul made the point that we are no longer tied to the Law. *"Since you died with Christ to the elemental spiritual forces of this world, why, as though you still belonged to the world, do you submit to its rules: 'Do not handle! Do not taste! Do not touch!'? These rules, which have to do with things that are all destined to perish with use, are based on merely human commands and teachings. Such regulations indeed have an appearance of wisdom, with their self-imposed worship, their false humility and their harsh treatment of the body, but they lack any value in restraining sensual indulgence"* (Colossians 2:20-23).

Christians throughout the world, having been misled by their church leaders, act as if Jesus' sacrifice was not enough. I believe that we dishonour Jesus' death when we try to atone for our sins by extra prayers or promises in exchange for His forgiveness, effectively saying that Jesus lied when He said that our sins have been atoned for once and for all.

Salvation

Here are some verses on the subject of salvation:

"For all have sinned and fall short of the glory of God" (Romans 3:23).

"For the wages of sin is death, but the gift of God is eternal life in Christ Jesus our Lord" (Romans 6:23).

"For God so loved the world that He gave His one and only Son, that whoever believes in Him shall not perish but have eternal life" (John 3:16).

"If you declare with your mouth, 'Jesus is Lord', and believe in your heart that God raised Him from the dead, you will be saved" (Romans 10:9).

"Yet to all who did receive Him, to those who believed in His name, He gave the right to become children of God" (John 1:12).

"For it is by grace you have been saved, through faith – and this not from yourselves, it is the gift of God – not by works, so that no one can boast" (Ephesians 2:8-9).

"The Word became flesh and made His dwelling among us. We have seen His glory, the glory of the one and only Son, who came from the Father, full of grace and truth" (John 1:14).

Salvation is, quite simply, a gift. There's no need to strive for it. In fact, there is no point in striving for it, because you will never attain it that way. It is not enough to believe that God exists. *"You believe that there is one God. Good! Even the demons believe that – and shudder"* (James 2:19). Jesus died only when He had completed the job His Father had given Him. The word 'finished' in the following verse has a sense of completion.

"When He had received the drink, Jesus said, 'It is finished.' With that, He bowed His head and gave up His Spirit" (John 19:30).

The late Billy Graham's son, Franklin Graham, clearly does not understand what it is like to be a gay Christian. In fact, he said that there is no such person as a 'gay Christian'. In April 2019, he wrote:

> A few days ago I posted about the South Bend, Indiana, Mayor Pete Buttigieg who says he is a gay Christian, married to a man. It generated a lot of interest as well as controversy.
>
> It is important to understand what 'repentance' and 'sin' mean. Sin is anything we do that is against God's commands. The Bible says that we are all guilty of sin – every person. God has put the entire human race under a death sentence because of man's sins. But God loves us and has provided a way of escape. He sent His Son Jesus Christ to earth to take our sins to the cross. He took our punishment on Himself, died on the cross, was buried, and by the power of Almighty God was raised to life on the third day.
>
> Whether you're the mayor of South Bend, the president of the United States Donald J. Trump, Franklin Graham, or anyone else – it doesn't matter who you are or what you have done – we're all guilty and need God's forgiveness. God is willing to forgive our sins if we will repent (turn from those sins, leave them, go the other direction).
>
> If we turn our back on Jesus Christ and such a wonderful salvation, and continue to live in our sins and don't repent, God will have no choice but to condemn us to an eternity separated from Him at the judgement.

My prayer for you reading this is that you will make the decision today to turn away from your sins, ask for God's forgiveness, and put your faith in His Son, Jesus Christ. I'm not condemning anyone, I'm not the judge, I don't make the rules – God does. And His rules are spelled out clearly in His Word, the Bible. It's up to each person to decide for themselves what their response to a loving God will be.

Franklin Graham needs to go back to the Bible and learn what it really says about sin and salvation. If his comment that everyone who continues to live in sin will be condemned to Hell were correct, there would not be a single person in the world who would be saved. In that writing, Graham proved that he does not understand the concept of grace.

Incidentally, Graham has not only taken an inordinate interest in politics, but demonstrated a complete lack of common sense when he spoke out the day after a group of Republicans joined the Democrats in charging Donald Trump with 'incitement of insurrection': *"Shame, shame on the ten Republicans who joined with Speaker Nancy Pelosi and the Democrats in impeaching President Trump yesterday. After all that he has done for our country, you would turn your back and betray him so quickly? We have never had a president like him in my lifetime"*.

****

Do we even care any more what the Bible says? Who bothers to read it, anyway? It may be the most popular book that has ever been published, but I believe that it is not nearly as popular as it used to be. God's written Word has been usurped by **Facebook** and other social websites.

A Nielsen survey in the US in 2018 revealed that *"American adults spend more than eleven hours per day watching, reading, listening to or simply interacting with media"*. Yet the total amount of old-style reading by Americans is on average only 16.8 minutes per day! Another survey in the US found that fewer than 20 per cent of church-goers actually read their Bible daily. How can you have a relationship with God if you don't even want to listen to what He might be saying to you?

For many years after I became a Christian I feared the day when I would arrive at God's Judgement Seat, expecting that my whole life – including the unsavoury parts, of which I am now deeply ashamed – would be replayed on a giant screen for all to see.

I now know, without the slightest doubt, that God has forgotten my sins. When I do front up to the Judgement Seat, I will be judged – and rewarded – only on the basis of what I did for the Kingdom of God while I was on Earth, not on my sins.

What a liberating truth that is. The Holy Spirit lives within me, to convict me not of sin, but of righteousness. Knowing that makes me want to *not* sin, whereas I found it impossible to be good when I felt that everything I did was under scrutiny. I learned that willpower alone is no match for the schemes of Satan.

Don't kid yourself that being straight will somehow earn you extra brownie points for your passage to Heaven. *Nothing* you do, however noble and unselfish you may be, will buy you that ticket. There is only one door, and Jesus holds the key to it.

Love

> ***And now these three remain: Faith, hope and love. But the greatest of these is love.***
> **1 Corinthians 13:13**

All 66 books of the Bible comprise God's *Love Story* to us.

John described himself twice in the gospel bearing his name as *"the disciple whom Jesus loved"* (John 13:23; 19:26). Although it took me decades to realise it, I am also *the disciple whom Jesus loves*. I think that is an important concept for us to understand, if we are really going to enter into a DPR with Jesus. He loves you as if you were His only child.

On 3 July 2019, in my daily chat with the Lord before getting out of bed, I told Him that I just could not understand the depth of His love for me. How could I even begin to understand the real meaning of what God said in John 3:16, that He *"so loved the world"*? We talk about unconditional love between members of a family, but what does real unconditional love look like? We have an idea from Jesus' amazing sacrifice on the cross, but it is still something I can't get my mind across. Incidentally, David said much the same thing in Psalm 139:6: *"Such knowledge is too wonderful for me, too lofty for me to attain"*.

God helped me in this understanding that same morning. The first online devotional I received after my observation about God's love for me was by Doctor Charles Stanley. Titled **God's Unfailing Love**, of course it captured my attention immediately! Talking about Ephesians 2:1-7, Charles said:

> <u>Do you feel loved by God?</u> [my emphasis] Let me ask the question a different way: Did you know that as a believer, it's possible to mentally understand God loves you without actually sensing it? In fact, the reverse can be true as well – we may say we love God, all the while knowing that our feelings of affection for Him are limited.
>
> There are a variety of reasons that a Christian might not sense love from God or affection for Him, some of which stem from childhood experiences. Perhaps love was absent in the home, or maybe it just wasn't expressed verbally or demonstrated in practical ways. An individual's personality could also be part of the equation – some people are naturally expressive while others are more reserved in their emotions.
>
> Although this discrepancy between knowledge and experience can be distressing, there is hope. <u>Meditating on all the ways God has demonstrated His love for you – and asking Him to help you perceive it – can begin to move that truth from your head to your heart</u> [my emphasis]. Remember that love is God's very nature (1 John 4:8), not something conditioned on your performance. And if you've been adopted into His family through faith in His Son, God has chosen to lavish kindness on you in Christ.
>
> Believing and accepting that you are loved by the Father will in turn affect your feelings for Him. Commit to knowing Him more intimately and accurately through His Word, and your affection for Him will begin to grow. As you spend time with Him in Scripture and prayer, you'll discover that the saying 'to know him is to love him' is certainly true of God."

Grace

This word hit me like a sledgehammer in October 1977. I suddenly realised that God did not expect me to earn my place in Heaven – and that it was something I couldn't do on my own, anyway, despite my best efforts. It means *unmerited favour*, and it showed me just how much God loves me. This is the crux of the whole salvation thing: The only way we can get to Heaven is through Jesus, who paid the penalty for our sins, thus enabling us to approach God's throne in the absolute assurance that we are perfect in His sight.

I make no apology for my ruthless attack on today's Church. Somehow the concept of *faith plus works* has crept into mainstream theology, as if our good works will help make us right with God. It is Jesus' good works, not ours, that will get us into Heaven.

Forgiveness

Many Christians seem to suffer from a fear that God has not forgiven them. More often than not, it's a fear that, because they continue to sin after accepting Jesus' penalty for their sin at the time of salvation, they may lose that salvation. Sure, the Holy Spirit convicts us when we sin, causing us to feel uncomfortable and guilty. But when we disobey God, our fellowship with Him is disrupted, causing us to lose the peace and joy that our relationship with Him had previously given us. <u>But God has forgiven us once and for all.</u> We can tell Him that we're sorry for having blown it once again, but we need to realise that we don't need Him to forgive us. Jesus' last words on the cross, *"It is finished"* (John 19:30), mean exactly that. He paid the penalty for our sins – past, present and future. It was a once-only event.

Christians need to know that they are forgiven. There is nothing we can do that will make God love us more, and nothing we have done that would make Him love us less. There is so much freedom in that truth.

The Anglican Church in Australia has a *confession* segment in its weekly liturgy. I don't know if the writers of it intended to do this, but it conveys the impression that we need to seek Jesus' forgiveness on a regular basis, as if the sins we had committed since our last confession were as yet unforgiven. This is an extension of what I have written about *sacrifices*.

You don't have to go to Confession every week to remain God's beloved child. Would you say to your infant son or daughter when they do something naughty, "Get out of my home! You're no child of mine!"?

When did Jesus pay the penalty for my sins? When He died. In other words, He paid the penalty for all my sins before I was even born!

Holiness

God is certainly holy. This is the whole reason why He cannot allow unforgiven sinners into His Heaven. Heaven would no longer be a holy place if He did.

It's hard for us to understand that a loving God would allow people to go to Hell. As I've said elsewhere in this book, God does not *send* anyone to Hell. That is something people choose for themselves. God created a way out for us when He allowed His precious Son to be nailed to a cross. But God is holy, and He simply cannot go against His own character and not exact punishment on anyone who fails to accept His free offer of forgiveness.

It is also hard for us to understand how a loving God can cause, or even just allow, suffering. Philip Yancey, writing in **Our Daily Bread** on 22 January 2017, had some wise comments about this issue:

"Why does a tornado hit one town and skip over another? Why do prayers for physical healing go unanswered?" Philip went on to say that he has learned to not even attempt to give people an answer to the *why* questions. But then he goes on: *"One question, however, no longer gnaws at me as it once did: 'Does God care?'. I know of only one way to answer that question, and the answer is Jesus. In Jesus, God gave us a face. If you wonder how God feels about the suffering on this groaning planet, look at that face".*

Compassion

Quoting the Lord's pronouncement to Moses in Exodus 33:19, Paul writes in his letter to the Romans:

"I will have mercy on whom I have mercy, and I will have compassion on whom I have compassion" (Romans 9:15).

Jesus had compassion on me, even as He hung on the Cross – and despite the fact that I had put Him there. It's not easy for us to treat with compassion those who wrong us, but Jesus gave us an example to follow. If anyone had reason to be bitter, it was He.

CHAPTER 5

What Do You Need to Do Now?

Love the Lord your God with all your heart and with all your soul and with all your mind.
Matthew 22:37

As a Christian, I have been set apart for God. I've been called to a higher love than I could ever experience with another human being. Jesus is my first love, and He should be yours, too.

You may think I am misusing my time when I spend two to three hours each morning with the Lord, and follow this up with other sessions later in the day. Shouldn't I be using this time to serve God through helping other people? Of course I have an obligation to use the talents and gifts I have been given to help people who are lacking in material blessings. The King James Version of the Bible translates Luke 12:48 in a way that has been used not just in a spiritual sense, but in countless situations regarding sharing of material assets: *"For unto whomsoever much is given, of him shall be much required"*.

But my primary purpose is a spiritual one. In fact, this book came about as a result of my passion to reach people for Jesus. When it's all said and done, that is all that matters. Jesus said, *"... whoever loses their life for My sake will find it"* (Matthew 10:39). I want everyone in my sphere of influence to find life, if they haven't already done so. For those who have found life, I want them to remember what Jesus said: *"I have come that they may have life, and have it to the full"* (John 10:10).

Once you transcend the very human desires that you have cultivated over many years, life takes on a whole new perspective. It is like you are on a completely new plane, far above the futile cares of this world. I can now understand what the King of Jerusalem[39] meant when he wrote the book of Ecclesiastes:

"The words of the Teacher, son of David, king in Jerusalem: 'Meaningless! Meaningless!' says the Teacher. 'Utterly meaningless! Everything is meaningless'" (Ecclesiastes 1:1-2).

I hasten to add here that worldly cares do still get in the way for me sometimes, but the realisation that my relationship with God is *all* that matters was very liberating. Everything I have here on Earth will eventually be stripped away. *"Naked I came from my mother's womb, and naked I will depart"* (Job 1:21). But I frequently have to remind myself of that truth, especially when I feel overwhelmed by circumstances.

If you are a straight Christian, I beg you to reach out to all the gay people you know – and there are sure to be a lot, both within your extended family and among your friends and associates – and let them know how much God loves them. Don't tell them that they need to change who they are for God to accept them. He accepts them exactly as they are, in the same way that He accepted you, with all your faults.

Acknowledge that Jesus Has Paid the Penalty for Your Sins

Let me ask you two questions:

1. If you were to die tonight, do you know for certain that you would go to Heaven?
2. If you were to die tonight and, finding yourself at the Judgement Seat of God, He were to ask you, *"Why should I let you into My Heaven?"*, what would you say?

---

[39] Until recently it was assumed that Ecclesiastes was written by King Solomon, (whose net worth was estimated in 2016, adjusted for inflation, to be the equivalent of 2.2 trillion US dollars!). Some modern scholars reject this, however, although it is likely that it was authored by a king of Jerusalem.

These are challenging questions. They are meant to be. God loves you more than you could possibly imagine – and proved it when He sent His own Son to die for you, so that you could become His child too.

What is a Christian? A Christian is someone who has recognised that they are a sinner by nature, and who has realised that Jesus alone can cleanse them of that sin. After 45 years as a Christian, I still have to pinch myself sometimes when I think about what Jesus did to make me acceptable to the Father. And all I had to do was ask for Jesus' forgiveness for my sin – once!

Love God and Others

As if the First Commandment etched into a stone tablet by God Himself was not enough, Jesus had to explain it again to a Pharisee who was trying to test Him, and I quote it once more here: *"Jesus replied: 'Love the Lord your God with all your heart and with all your soul and with all your mind.' This is the first and greatest commandment. And the second is like it: 'Love your neighbour as yourself'. All the Law and the Prophets hang on these two commandments"* (Matthew 22:37-40).

Perhaps the Pharisee didn't understand the meaning of the First Commandment given by God on the stone tablet. I suspect that many of us today also don't get it. God was not talking about having an each-way bet, as many people did back in those days. Paul referred to this when he addressed the Greeks at the *Aeropagus* in Athens, saying he could see that they worshipped many gods:

"For as I walked around and looked carefully at your objects of worship, I even found an altar with this inscription: TO AN UNKNOWN GOD. So you are ignorant of the very thing you worship – and this is what I am going to proclaim to you" (Acts 17:23).

No, God wasn't just telling His people not to worship the Roman and Greek gods to whom the people made sacrifices in order to keep in their good books. Jesus made it very clear what God meant when he addressed the Pharisee. <u>We are called to love God above everything else.</u> If we're honest with ourselves, we'll realise that we, too, have created our own gods. Wealth, status, hedonistic pleasures, sex and even family can displace God as the most important reality in our lives. And He doesn't just demand to be at the top of the bill in our list of gods; He demands that He be the *only* item on it. That is not to say that we can't continue to cherish good things, such as family and friends, but they must not be objects of worship. The Uniting Church I used to attend in Canberra conducted a survey. One of the questions was: *"Is God your most important reality?"* Only 28 per cent of the people who had responded to the survey said that He was. When I asked an office-bearer some time later whether she could attest to that herself, she replied candidly that she couldn't – that her family was more important to her than God.

I suspect it's thinking like hers that is behind the dread that almost everyone has of dying. I have known Christians who, despite being in intense suffering in the final stages of their lives, were extremely reluctant to let go. When I asked one lovely Christian man recently why he felt this way, especially since he knew that his suffering would end the moment he went to be with Jesus, he said that he didn't want to leave his family. There was clearly a fear of the unknown there as well.

Simply Trust Him

"The boundary lines have fallen for me in pleasant places; surely I have a delightful inheritance. I will praise the Lord, who counsels me; even at night my heart instructs me. I keep my eyes always on the Lord. With Him at my right hand, I will not be shaken" (Psalm 16:6-8).

God wants you to trust Him for absolutely everything. He can see what you can't: The future! When you were a child, your parents would take your hand when danger lurked, such as crossing a busy road. They knew the risks of letting you go off on your own. God is like that. He wants you to hold His hand as He helps you navigate the murky waters of life.

When Peter saw Jesus walking on the water, he asked Jesus to tell him to come to Him on the water. *"Come, He said"* (Matthew 14:29). Trusting Jesus, Peter stepped out of the boat and walked on the water's surface towards Jesus. So far, so good. But then he looked around him, rather than at Jesus, and began to sink. That is a great lesson for us today. If we keep our eyes firmly focused on Jesus, and not on the surrounding circumstances that threaten to engulf us, He will ensure that we don't sink.

I love this old song:

> Turn your eyes upon Jesus
> Look full in His wonderful face
> And the things of Earth will grow strangely dim
> In the light of His glory and grace.

He Wants, and Demands, All of You

You shall have no other gods before Me.
Exodus 20:3

But this is not a requirement for salvation!

While the saying is true that nothing we have done would make God love us less and nothing we could do would make Him love us more, God does expect total commitment from us. I believe this is for our benefit, not His.

A pig and a chicken are walking down the road. The chicken says: *"Hey Pig, I was thinking we should open a restaurant!"* Pig replies: *"Hm, maybe. What would we call it?"* The chicken responds: *"How about 'Ham-n-Eggs'?"* The pig thinks for a moment and says: *"No thanks. I'd be committed, but you'd only be involved"*.

Kirsten Holmberg said in **Our Daily Bread** on 2 December 2017: *"As we face our own battles and challenges, let's remember that God is our best ally. He strengthens us when we're willing to 'serve up' a whole-hearted commitment to Him"*.

One of the contributors to **Gospel Transformation Notes**[40] said about Ephesians 4:20: *"When we embraced Christ and received him, it was not to continue on in the same futile ways of thinking. If our lives do not differ from the lives of unbelievers, we have not truly learned of Christ. When Christ calls us to himself it is always a call to leave the world, die to self, and live for God. Let us never accept a false gospel which says we can have Jesus as Saviour without also having him as Lord. It must be both or neither"*.

---

[40] © 2013 by Crossway

God wants you more than He wants your work. While He wants your gifts of service, your worship of Him is far more important to Him – and to you. The Lord made this very clear to me on 28 January 2017, when I asked Him to encourage me as I faced the giants on the path to what I call my Big Dream.

My first devotional for the day (in **Our Daily Bread**) was by Randy Kilgore, who said, *"we serve a God who loves us more than our work"*. That was not exactly what I had wanted to hear, but it made me realise that God doesn't need me to fulfil His purposes. All I have to do is give myself to Him fully.

But the encouragement I had been looking for came in the first online message by Joseph Prince later in my quiet time. In view of the word 'giants' that I had used in my prayer before getting out of bed that morning, the title of the message certainly got my attention: **See Your Giants as Bread**! Prince then quoted a verse from the Old Testament: *"… do not … fear the people [giants] of the land, for they are our bread; their protection has departed from them, and the Lord is with us. Do not fear them"* (Numbers 14:9). He went on to say: *"When you see a 'giant' today in your business, health or ministry, I challenge you to see it as bread that will only make you stronger"*.

God created us with marvellous uniqueness and the awesome ability to have an intimate relationship with Him.

I read in **Time with God** on 1 February 2019: *"Soak yourself in the Scriptures. God will speak to you through them and help you understand His ways. The Bible will show you how you can live in a way that allows God to work in and through you. Author Kay Arthur says, 'I believe the greater the pressure, the greater your need for time alone with Him'"*.

"But we have this treasure in jars of clay to show that this all-surpassing power is from God and not from us" (2 Corinthians 4:7).

Kirsten Holmberg again wrote in **Our Daily Bread** of 11 January 2018: *"Paul describes the truth of Jesus' life, death and resurrection as a treasure, carried about in the frail humanity of God's people. That treasure enables those who trust in Him to bear up under unthinkable adversity and continue in their service. When they do, His light – His life – shines brightly through the 'cracks' of their humanness. Paul encourages us all not to 'lose heart' (2 Corinthians 4:16) because God strengthens us to do His work … When God's *strength shines through us, it invites others to ask, 'What's inside?'. We can then unzip our hearts and reveal the life-giving promise of salvation in Christ".*

As I said, God wants all of you, not just a part. He wants you to be obedient. He may call you to give extra money to the church or to someone in need. He may even, as with the rich young man who asked Jesus what he had to do to inherit eternal life (Matthew 19:16-22), tell you to give up *everything*. There are no fixed rules, even though most churches continue to peddle misinformation about tithing, misinterpreting Malachi 3:10. Don't – *please* don't – put Jesus into a neat little box.

Many Christians are happy to acknowledge that God is a part of their lives; but, like the woman I spoke of earlier in this chapter, they admit their families are more important to them than God. But God doesn't want to be just a part of our life: He demands, and deserves, to *be* our life. When you surrender every part of your being to Him, you are not bound. On the contrary, you become free for the first time in your life. If you are bent on hanging on to your material possessions, just remember this: At the end of the game, all the toys have to go back into the box.

Maybe you don't even realise that you have need of salvation. You believe that you are in no immediate danger of dying, so you have no need just now for a Saviour. But your life could be snuffed out at any time, maybe even today. The bad news is that, if you die without having surrendered your life to Jesus, you *will* go to Hell. Please don't put off that decision for another moment!

"I no longer live, but Christ lives in me" (Galatians 2:20). Hardly a minute passes when I am not thinking about God. That might seem extreme to you, but if you were sitting alongside your earthly father, wouldn't it be natural for you to chat with him often? You wouldn't save up all your thoughts for one particular time of the day, would you? In the same way, I chat with my Father whenever anything comes into my mind. For example, when we were staying in a hotel in May 2019, it rained heavily on our last night there – even though no rain had been expected for at least the next five days. When I thanked God for the rain – which I just love to hear, as long as I'm snug and warm inside – He said that He brought it to wash our car! I had been thinking how dirty it was, and that I would at least have to wash the windscreen before we headed

off for the long drive home. Had I not had such a DPR with my Lord, I might have missed that little miracle.

Express Gratitude

Did you know that Jesus said only ten per cent of people express gratitude? When He healed ten lepers, you would have expected that all of them would have returned to thank Him. But only one did! That might seem incredible to you, but isn't that how most of us are? We have so much to thank Jesus for, yet we just don't do it.

Life is too busy for most of us to even take time to smell the roses. Yet we are blessed every day, in many ways. Even if you can't stop by that rose bush, you can still thank God for its beauty as you walk or run past it. I can't help thanking God many times throughout the day for something He has just blessed me with, though I suspect there are countless other blessings that I just take for granted.

The Americans have commemorated Thanksgiving since 1621, when, over three days, the Pilgrim Fathers thanked God for their harvest. These days Thanksgiving is always celebrated on the last Thursday in November. It is a great opportunity to thank God for His blessings. But I believe the whole world would be a better place if we all celebrated Thanksgiving – every day. Every good gift we have is from God, who loves us more than anyone.

Living with an *attitude of gratitude* has amazing benefits for us as well. It gives us a sense of peace. It does away with the feeling that if we could just have that one extra thing we would be happy. On a global level, I believe that exercising gratitude constantly would prevent wars, convince those with plenty to feed the billions who are starving, and draw us closer to God.

Freedom within Boundaries

When I was a small boy I was allowed to play anywhere on our property. In those days, I was even allowed to wander up the hill to our neighbours' homes. When I was four, I used to walk up to the top of the hill where we lived and knock on the kitchen door of a lovely lady. She told me many years later that, unable to speak English at that time, I would hold my hand out and say *"Sjokolade"*, which is Norwegian for chocolate. I actually remember it, though I don't recall that I said it in Norwegian. While I had a lot of freedom to wander around in those days, I was not permitted to play on the road. My parents had to set boundaries for me. Those boundaries never seemed to interfere with my freedoms, and I just accepted them as being something put in place for my own safety.

Similarly, God has given me boundaries, also for my safety. Sadly, though, I haven't always respected those boundaries, to my own shame and pain. When I started to live as a gay man, it seemed that all the boundaries had been removed. I was free to do whatever I wanted. Giving little or no thought to my own welfare, or to that of others, I completely ignored God's clear instructions in the Bible. It was like Adam and Eve all over again. Eve was convinced by the serpent – Satan – that her eyes would be opened in a new way, if only she were to eat the fruit from the one tree that was forbidden to her and Adam. God had set boundaries for them, but Eve, and then Adam, decided to flout them. Their own pride and selfish desires were their downfall. Their sin has affected every person born since then. My own ignoring of the boundaries that God has set may not affect every person on Earth, but it has certainly hurt many people.

I realised long ago that God does not reveal sin in my life in order to condemn me, but to restore me to fellowship with Him and to help me reconcile with those I have hurt. Repentance clears the way for renewed closeness with God. It's not that He has pushed me away, but that I have hidden from him, much as Adam and Eve hid from God in the Garden of Eden when they realised that they were naked.

You are not alone, so don't try to do life on your own. Whatever mountain you have to climb, do it while you hold Jesus' hand.

What Does God Expect of You?

The Church has put expectations on its followers that God never intended. It seems to have a list of sins that God needs them to deal with before He will be prepared to walk in fellowship with them. Some churches even maintain that God will not forgive someone who persists in committing the same sin over and over, even if they ask Him for forgiveness each time. Unless they repent (that is, turn away from their sin), they say, there won't be any forgiveness.

God certainly expects you to at least try to follow the principles enunciated in the Ten Commandments, even though He knows you will fail constantly. But such expectations have no conditions attached. He will never condemn someone who has accepted Jesus' gift of salvation.

And this brings me to God's only expectation, with a promise that you can take to the bank: If you acknowledge that you are a sinner who has no hope of getting to Heaven by your own works, and that Jesus paid the penalty for your failures, you *will* have eternal life.

Churches seem very happy to tell you to remove the splinter from your eye, while ignoring the log in their own eye.

God knows you will continue to sin. If you suffer from some sort of addiction, you will persist in committing the same sin over and over unless and until you are delivered from that addiction. But every one of us sins, every day.

On Pottery

Yet you, Lord, are our Father. We are the clay, you are the potter; we are all the work of your hand
Isaiah 64:8

A Broken Pot

I have often felt regret for the mistakes I've made, thinking my life could have been a lot less painful if I had allowed the Lord to guide me, especially at important crossroads. The pain I have caused to the people I love has also been a real thorn in my flesh. But, when I reached the grand age of seventy, God told me something that made all the pain go away: *"It doesn't matter how you got here, but you are now where I want you"*. As I look back on all the hardships and the – mostly self-inflicted – pain, I wonder if I would have got to where I am now if things had been different. As I keep saying, nothing, absolutely nothing, is as important as having a DPR with Jesus.

Being moulded into the person Jesus wants me to be

Life is a process. If we let it, it will be a process of refinement, as God moulds us into the people He wants us to be. Too often, however, we are just happy to be who we are. Change is simply too difficult.

While I believe I am much more complete now than I used to be, most of my family and friends know that there's a lot more moulding and polishing still to be done. Sometimes God has to break off a bit that hasn't formed as it should, and He has to start again with that part. While I may not like what is happening, I know now that resistance is futile. The process won't be complete until Jesus comes to take me home. I am here for Him, not He for me.

Prayer of Response

If you would like to accept Jesus as your Saviour, with all the benefits that accrue from being a member of the 'Royal Family', the following prayer taken from a booklet by Vic Jakopson titled **Just Grace** is all you need to say.

> My Lord and my God,
> I have lived my life, my way.
> I have done many wrong things.
> I repent of all my sin.
> Please forgive me.
> I trust You now to be my Saviour.
> Thank You for dying in my place.
> I ask You now for Your gift of eternal life.
> I give my life to You
> And want You to be my Lord.
> Help me to live for You
> By the power of Your Holy Spirit.
> These things I pray in Jesus' name.
> Amen.

CHAPTER 6

A Glorious Future

'For I know the plans I have for you,' declares the Lord, 'plans to prosper you and not to harm you, plans to give you hope and a future'.
Jeremiah 29:11

Life Here and Now

The 19th century philosopher, Henry Thoreau, said that *"the mass of men lead lives of quiet desperation"*. Perhaps his observation was correct, but it doesn't need to be that way.

Jesus said: *"I have come that they may have life, and have it to the full"* (John 10:10). He wants your life to have purpose, and promises peace and joy to all who turn to Him. That is not to say that you won't suffer any more, but He assures you that He is always with you in the storms of life.

God is not a killjoy

Well before I became a Christian, I met a guy who, when confronted with making a decision to follow Jesus, said that he first wanted to enjoy life. It seems ironic that life's enjoyment is incomparably enhanced when we are walking with the Lord!

Perhaps with the same thought – that life would cease to be enjoyable for him if he were to commit to becoming a Christian – a young truck driver who had asked to be married in our Anglican church in Sydney told our Minister that he was not yet ready to make that decision. The Minister warned him that there was no certainty he would get another opportunity. A few days later the man was killed in an accident in his truck.

John North wrote the following devotional in his daily **Time with God** for 5 December 2018:

> Life is best for those who live it God's way! A spiritual perspective on life is so different from the world's perspective. The world looks at a person who bases his life on the Word of God – who lives by God's principles and does what is right – and thinks, 'How boring! What a waste! He should be enjoying life!' But if you have ever walked God's way in life, you know that those days lived in close fellowship with God, sensing his pleasure over your life, were the best part of your life. People who base their lives around themselves, who live for wealth and their own advantage, end up with huge amounts of stress in their lives. They are constantly anxious about so many things. But the person who builds his life around God's Word experiences peace, even when crises come, because he knows that God takes responsibility for the life of the person who honours Him. Today God is challenging you to change your perspective on godliness. Godliness is not only the right way to live, it is the BEST way to live! God wants the best for you.

Paul wrote in Ephesians 3:20 that God *"is able to do immeasurably more than all we ask or imagine, according to His power that is at work within us"*. I believe this means that the supernatural can become natural for us if we allow God to act in and through us. I've seen it time after time in my own life, and there is no reason why you shouldn't see it in your own life as well.

What's the Point?

My good friend, the late James Pegler, first recorded **Let Me Choose Life** on his album, ***James Pegler***, in 1971. I still have the album that he gave me. At the time, I was not a Christian (though James was), but the song had a profound impact on me. I wondered if my life had any point, and it was another six years before I discovered that it did. Here are the opening words to the song, which were actually said without music:

To be born, to grow up
To grow older, to grow old
Endlessly pursuing a petty pot of gold

> *At the end of a plastic rainbow.*
> *And then to die, beneath a neon-coloured sky*
> *Having found that the pot was empty, and it's too late to cry.*
> *Is that all life has in store?*
> *Isn't there anything more?*

I don't think I have ever believed that this life is all there is, but I remember the song made me think about the futility of the life that most people choose. While it was a secular song, it had a strong Christian message. If you choose life, you have something amazing to look forward to!

I Believe Everyone Has a 'Big Dream'

What is your Big Dream? Do you still have it, or has it been forgotten because it all seemed too hard? Remember that God has a purpose for every one of His precious children. Sometimes, however, He gives us a new dream, completely contrary to the one we had been pursuing.

The Old Testament is full of examples of broken people, just like you and me, whom God used mightily to advance His Kingdom. And who could forget the New Testament heroes, especially Paul, whose paths were literally blocked by God, so He could steer them on another course? Paul – or Saul as he was known as at that time – was such a devout Jew that he was determined to wipe out Christianity by getting rid of its followers. That was *his* Big Dream. However, on his way to Damascus to have the Christians there arrested and brought back to Rome, God intervened in a spectacular way. Saul was struck blind, and given a new Big Dream by God.

Most of us don't experience such a stupendous intervention by God as Saul did – and our big dream may not have such a huge impact on the world as the one God gave to Saul – but whatever dream God has given you, I urge you to pursue it with all the talents He has given you. Douglas Malloch's poem, **Be the Best of Whatever You Are**, has always encouraged me, especially when I've observed with envy the impact that other Christians have had:

> *If you can't be a pine on the top of the hill,*
> *Be a scrub in the valley – but be*

> *The best little scrub by the side of the rill;*
> *Be a bush if you can't be a tree.*
> *If you can't be a bush be a bit of the grass,*
> *And some highway happier make;*
> *If you can't be a muskie then just be a bass –*
> *But the liveliest bass in the lake!*
> *We can't all be captains, we've got to be crew,*
> *There's something for all of us here,*
> *There's big work to do, and there's lesser to do,*
> *And the task you must do is the near.*
> *If you can't be a highway then just be a trail,*
> *If you can't be the sun be a star;*
> *It isn't by size that you win or you fail –*
> *Be the best of whatever you are!"*

Death

Statistically, 100 out of every 100 people will die. So why is death such a taboo topic?

Fear

When we were infants and our parents took us somewhere we had never been before, we were not at all afraid. We knew how much our parents loved us, and that they would never allow us to come into harm's way. Why don't Christians have that same trust in our Heavenly Father? As kids, we thought our parents were all-powerful and that they knew everything. As adult Christians, we can have that same confidence, but in our Father in Heaven. I want to impart that confidence to people who are dying, so that they can actually look forward to leaving this life and being with the Lord forever.

Death brings new life

Death is not the end. It is the beginning! This life is brief, as older people can testify. The Roman philosopher, Seneca, had some amazing insights into the human psyche. One of his sayings has stayed in my mind for many years:

"We are always complaining that our days are few, and acting as though there would be no end to them".

Most people are not quite happy with life, but they are terrified that it could end before they're ready.

As I have said before, I am really looking forward to the next life. It's what I was created for. I have my ticket; my bags are packed. I have only to leave a note for the milkman.

End Times

The Rapture

You've probably heard Christians talk about the Rapture, and how they can't wait for it to happen. I subscribe to the dispensational pre-millennialist view that this event will happen prior to the Great Tribulation. But that could just be my wishful thinking. I have no desire to be stuck on Earth during the seven years[41] when the Antichrist will rule. Under the dispensational, pre-millennialist scenario, all living Christians will be lifted up into the sky – *before* the Antichrist takes over the world – where they will be joined by the bodies of all those believers who had died beforehand. I find the concept of that absolutely thrilling. Here one moment; gone the next!

You don't want to be one of those who are left behind. Incidentally, the **Left Behind** books by Tim LaHaye and Jerry B Jenkins, while fictional, give a really dramatic interpretation of what might happen following the Rapture.

---

[41] Most theologians believe this to be the actual number of years that the Antichrist will rule, though he will only show his true colours in the second half of that period.

The Great Tribulation

The Great Tribulation will be a short period when the Antichrist, a man appointed by Satan himself to rule the Earth, causes all manner of calamities to befall the people who have been left behind. God will allow this to happen, giving them a chance to turn to Jesus before it's too late. The Antichrist will have many supernatural powers. The Tribulation will be a sort of second chance, where people who are not already Christians will be forced to decide whether to follow the Devil or Jesus. It will be a very clear choice.

Heaven

A close friend of mine, a Christian, said he's concerned that Heaven will be boring – a never-ending worship service. We will certainly have work to do, as we are told in Revelation 7:15: *"Therefore, they are before the throne of God and serve Him day and night in His temple"*. But Heaven will be anything but boring. The Bible has given us only a few tantalising glimpses of what we can expect there, and it's all good. And remember that time as we know it doesn't exist in the spiritual realm, so it's not going to be like sitting through a seemingly endless sermon.

Adoption

The adoption papers for all Christians have been signed and activated.

"But when the set time had fully come, God sent his Son, born of a woman, born under the law, to redeem those under the law, that we might receive adoption to sonship. Because you are his sons, God sent the Spirit of his Son into our hearts, the Spirit who calls out, 'Abba, Father.' So you are no longer a slave, but God's child; and since you are his child, God has made you also an heir" (Galatians 4:4-7).

The best is yet to be!

Jesus is coming back again, and possibly sooner than most of us would like. The good news is that, if you are a Christian, you have nothing to fear.

The prophetic book of Revelation, the last book in the Bible, is certainly not easy to understand. I doubt that anyone has ever really understood it. But it paints a picture of the glorious future you can expect, if and when you go to Heaven.

What is Heaven like?

As I write this, two elderly Christian friends of mine are facing the very real prospect of being taken home to Heaven in the next few months. Both of them, however, are reluctant to leave their lives here, even though they are suffering physically, all day every day. I'm having trouble understanding that. To me, it is simply a transition from one world to another. In their cases, it's giving up a life of pain and suffering in exchange for something that is too glorious to even imagine. It sounds wonderful!

As I pondered this conundrum, I thought of a story I heard about a mine worker. While he spends most of his life far beneath the Earth's surface, he does know that there is something much better above. His shift has just finished, and he should be taking the elevator up to the fresh air and sunshine. But he says he's comfortable down there, in more familiar surroundings. That would make no sense to most people, and it makes none to me, but it is exactly the mindset of many Christians who are suffering from debilitating terminal illness.

So why do Christians fear death? I believe it has everything to do with our relationship with Jesus. Do we really love Him as we say we do? Surely, if we walk with Him, metaphorically, every day on Earth, wouldn't the prospect of walking with Him physically be something that would excite us, rather than fill us with dread?

This is where we once again have to turn to Scripture.

"There is no fear in love. But perfect love drives out fear, because fear has to do with punishment. The one who fears is not made perfect in love" (1 John 4:18).

It is a physical place, where we will have physical – perfect! – bodies.

"But Christ has indeed been raised from the dead, the firstfruits of those who have fallen asleep. For since death came through a man, the resurrection of the dead comes also through a man" (1 Corinthians 15:20-21).

It has been described as *Utopia on Steroids*, a place of great joy. There will be no sickness, no hatred, no suffering, no pain.

We will be 'surrounded' by God.

It is eternal: *"Then they will go away to eternal punishment, but the righteous to eternal life"* (Matthew 25:46).

Do we go there as soon as we die?

Yes. I handed my son, David, over to Jesus on 14 May 1985. I know he was taken immediately to Heaven, certainly his soul. From what I can gather, the souls of Christians go immediately to be with the Father, though our bodies are not resurrected until Jesus comes again.

I recall hearing of a famous Christian who, with death imminent, was surrounded by his family. He had been silent, and with his eyes closed, for some time, when suddenly his eyes opened. *"You came personally?"*, he exclaimed. With that he was gone. I believe that he saw Jesus arrive to take him home.

"Just as people are destined to die once, and after that to face judgement, so Christ was sacrificed once to take away the sins of many; and he will appear a second time, not to bear sin, but to bring salvation to those who are waiting for him" (Hebrews 9:27-28).

"Jesus answered him, 'Truly I tell you, today you will be with me in paradise'" (Luke 23:43).

Hell

If you go to Hell, you will have only Satan and his demons to keep you company. You will be separated from all your loved ones, as well as from God. I recall an imagined conversation between God and someone who had found himself in Hell:

"Where is my family, Lord?"
"Not here".

"Where are my friends, Lord?"
"Not here".
"Where are You, Lord?"
"Not here".

Hell is a physical place. It has been described in the Bible as a "lake of fire": *"Anyone whose name was not found written in the book of life was thrown into the lake of fire"* (Revelation 20:15). But the scariest thing for me, as I said earlier, is that it is a place of *separation*.

In 1979 I went with my then-young nephew, Christian Cordeaux, to the opening night of the movie, **The Black Hole**. I have never liked science fiction movies, and this one was no exception. But the ending was one of the most frightening segments of fiction I've ever seen. It was so scary, in fact, that it seems the ending was dropped from a remake in 2006.

In the climax to the movie, the heroes' spaceship is sucked into the Black Hole, where the most amazing scene unfolds. Below them is a mass of stalagmites, surrounded by flames. On the top of each one is a person, screaming in anguish. Of course no one can hear them and, with the flames all around them, they can't even see each other. That, to me, is a perfect representation of Hell: Unbelievable anguish, made worse by the fact that there is absolutely no one around to provide comfort.

Make no mistake: The Bible is very clear about the fact that we will be called to account before the Creator of the Universe when we die.

Jesus offers us a way of escape from the horrible punishment that we all deserve. That is why He died. He paid the penalty for our sins – not just our past sins, but those we are committing right now, and even those we will commit in the future. I don't need to ask for His forgiveness, since, as I have pointed out, He has already 'forgotten' the sins I have committed.

Don't think you can get to Heaven under your own steam – you are just not good enough. God's standard is absolute perfection, and if you are not perfect you won't get in. After all, it wouldn't be Heaven if it were not perfect, would it?

This is why it is so important to appreciate what Jesus has done for us. Through His death we are made perfect. He was the ultimate *Sacrificial Lamb* that featured so much in the Old Testament. And, importantly, with Jesus' death on the Cross, the Old Covenant ceased to apply:

"So if the Son sets you free, you will be free indeed" (John 8:36).

****

I don't want anyone to end up in Hell, which is why I have written this book. If you have not yet accepted Jesus as your Saviour, I beg you to do so now, before it's too late. You never know when your time here will come to an end.

In conclusion, let me warn you that you *will* one day bow before the Lord, even if you have not acknowledged Him in this life:

"It is written: 'As surely as I live,' says the Lord, 'every knee will bow before Me; every tongue will acknowledge God'" (Romans 14:11).

Appendix

Extracts from the Roman Catholic Catechism

The Catechism is a document of 1,425 pages and is basically rules on how to be a Christian – proving that the Catholic Church has no idea what the Bible is really about.

1. Item 966 says that Jesus' mother, Mary, *"when the course of her earthly life was finished, was taken up body and soul into heavenly glory, and exalted by the Lord as Queen over all things…"*. That's certainly not in the Bible! That item also says to Mary: *"In giving birth you kept your virginity…"*. Catholics call Mary the 'Blessed Virgin', maintaining that she never lost her virginity, even though she gave birth naturally to a number of other children after Jesus.

2. Item 967. Still talking of Mary, the Catechism says, *"By her complete adherence to the Father's will …"*. Does that mean that Catholics believe Mary was without sin?

3. Item 971. *"From the most ancient times the Blessed Virgin has been honoured with the title 'Mother of God', to whose protection the faithful fly in all their dangers and needs …"*. Again, this is not from the Bible.

4. Item 975. *"We believe that the Holy Mother of God, the new Eve, Mother of the Church, continues in heaven to exercise her maternal role on behalf of the members of Christ"*. In their dreams!

5. Item 1023 (Heaven). *"Those who die in God's grace and friendship and are perfectly purified live for ever with Christ. They are like God for ever, for they 'see him as he is,' face to face: By virtue of our apostolic authority, we define the following: According to the general*

disposition of God, the souls of all the saints . . . and other faithful who died after receiving Christ's holy Baptism (provided they were not in need of purification when they died, . . . or, if they then did need or will need some purification, when they have been purified after death, . . .) already before they take up their bodies again and before the general judgment - and this since the Ascension of our Lord and Saviour Jesus Christ into heaven – have been, are and will be in heaven, in the heavenly Kingdom and celestial paradise with Christ, joined to the company of the holy angels. Since the Passion and death of our Lord Jesus Christ, these souls have seen and do see the divine essence with an intuitive vision, and even face to face, without the mediation of any creature"*. It's too late for 'purification' after a person has died. Hebrews 9:27 says that *"people are destined to die once, and after that to face judgement"*. This Catechism is reading more and more like a fairy tale!

6. Item 1030 (Purgatory). *"All who die in God's grace and friendship, but still imperfectly purified, are indeed assured of their eternal salvation; but after death they undergo purification, so as to achieve the holiness necessary to enter the joy of heaven"*. The notion of Purgatory is not even biblical.

7. Item 1031 (Purgatory still). *"The Church gives the name Purgatory to this final purification of the elect, which is entirely different from the punishment of the damned. ... As for certain lesser faults, we must believe that, before the Final Judgment, there is a purifying fire. He who is truth says that whoever utters blasphemy against the Holy Spirit will be pardoned neither in this age nor in the age to come. From this sentence we understand that certain offences can be forgiven in this age, but certain others in the age to come"*. The Catholic Church does not understand the meaning of the term 'blasphemy against the Holy Spirit'. The Bible verse[42] is simply talking of people who rejected Jesus in this life.

---

[42] *"And so I tell you, every kind of sin and slander can be forgiven, but blasphemy against the Spirit will not be forgiven"* (Matthew 12:31).

8. Item 1032 (Praying for the dead). *"This teaching is also based on the practice of prayer for the dead, already mentioned in Sacred Scripture:* <u>*'Therefore Judas Maccabeus made atonement for the dead, that they might be delivered from their sin'*</u> [my emphasis]. *From the beginning the Church has honoured the memory of the dead and offered prayers in suffrage for them, above all the Eucharistic sacrifice, so that, thus purified, they may attain the beatific vision of God.* <u>*The Church also commends almsgiving, indulgences*</u> [my emphasis], *and works of penance undertaken on behalf of the dead: Let us help and commemorate them. If Job's sons were purified by their father's sacrifice, why would we doubt that our offerings for the dead bring them some consolation? Let us not hesitate to help those who have died and to offer our prayers for them"*. There is no biblical basis for these assertions. Once again, the Catholic Church is relying on the Apocrypha to justify its outrageous claims. It is simply astounding that the Church has not been called out on the issue of Indulgences. "Give money to your church, so that your deceased loved one can be redeemed"!

9. Item 1033 (Hell). *"We cannot be united with God unless we freely choose to love him. But we cannot love God if we sin gravely against him, against our neighbour or against ourselves: 'He who does not love remains in death. Anyone who hates his brother is a murderer, and you know that no murderer has eternal life abiding in him.' Our Lord warns us that we shall be separated from him if we fail to meet the serious needs of the poor and the little ones who are his brethren. To die in mortal sin without repenting and accepting God's merciful love means remaining separated from him for ever by our own free choice. This state of definitive self-exclusion from communion with God and the blessed is called 'hell'"*. Talk about 'twisted scripture'!

10. Item 1068 is the crux of the Catholic Church's wrong beliefs regarding salvation. I think they would like to rewrite Ephesians 2:8 to say, "It is by <u>works</u> you have been saved, not just faith …". This item says: *"For it is in the liturgy* [defined as 'the participation of the People of God in the work of God']*, especially in the divine sacrifice of the*

Eucharist, that 'the work of our redemption is accomplished,' and it is through the liturgy especially that the faithful are enabled to express in their lives and manifest to others the mystery of Christ and the real nature of the true Church".

11. The Catholic Church believes that if an infant dies without having been baptised, it will go to Hell. Item 1250 says: *"Born with a fallen human nature and tainted by original sin, children also have need of the new birth in Baptism to be freed from the power of darkness and brought into the realm of the freedom of the children of God, to which all men are called. The sheer gratuitousness of the grace of salvation is particularly manifest in infant Baptism. The Church and the parents would deny a child the priceless grace of becoming a child of God were they not to confer Baptism shortly after birth"*. What happens if the child dies before a priest has a chance to baptise them? And woe betide anyone who doesn't help the baptised soul understand what is required of them as they get older. Item 1255 says: *"The whole ecclesial community bears some responsibility for the development and safeguarding of the grace given at Baptism"*. In other words, even though their ritual of infant baptism is supposed to save the child, grace may be lost if the child is not nurtured properly!

12. In Item 1257, the Catholic Church has exposed its complete failure to understand Jesus' command that people be baptised: *"The Lord himself affirms that Baptism is necessary for salvation. He also commands his disciples to proclaim the Gospel to all nations and to baptize them. Baptism is necessary for salvation for those to whom the Gospel has been proclaimed and who have had the possibility of asking for this sacrament. The Church does not know of any means other than Baptism that assures entry into eternal beatitude; this is why she takes care not to neglect the mission she has received from the Lord to see that all who can be baptized are 'reborn of water and the Spirit.' God has bound salvation to the sacrament of Baptism, but he himself is not bound by his sacraments"*. I explained in Chapter 3 what Jesus meant about baptism.

13. Item 1258. *"The Church has always held the firm conviction that those who suffer death for the sake of the faith without having received Baptism are baptized by their death for and with Christ. This Baptism of blood, like the desire for Baptism, brings about the fruits of Baptism without being a sacrament".* This sounds just like Islam: If you die a martyr – having killed a bunch of 'infidels', you are guaranteed a place in Paradise – along with 72 virgins!
14. Item 1259. *"For catechumens who die before their Baptism, their explicit desire to receive it, together with repentance for their sins, and charity, assures them the salvation that they were not able to receive through the sacrament".* I think they inserted that one to make sure people gave to the Church before they died!
15. The belief of the Catholic Church that salvation is achieved by both grace and works is the reason I think it is a complete mistake to call it a Christian church. Item 1949 says: *"Called to beatitude but wounded by sin, man stands in need of salvation from God. Divine help comes to him in Christ through the law that guides him and the grace that sustains him: Work out your own salvation with fear and trembling; for God is at work in you, both to will and to work for his good pleasure".*
16. Item 2333 (Sexuality). *"<u>Everyone, man and woman, should acknowledge and accept his sexual identity</u>* [my emphasis]. *Physical, moral, and spiritual difference and complementarity are oriented toward the goods of marriage and the flourishing of family life. The harmony of the couple and of society depends in part on the way in which the complementarity, needs, and mutual support between the sexes are lived out".* That's an interesting statement, especially in view of the fact that the Catholic Church acknowledges that people can be born gay!
17. Masturbation is banned by the Catholic Church. Item 2352 says, *"Both the Magisterium of the Church, in the course of a constant tradition, and the moral sense of the faithful have been in no doubt and have firmly maintained that masturbation is an intrinsically and gravely disordered action".*

18. As for homosexuality, Item 2357 says: *"Homosexuality refers to relations between men or between women who experience an exclusive or predominant sexual attraction toward persons of the same sex. It has taken a great variety of forms through the centuries and in different cultures. Its psychological genesis remains largely unexplained. Basing itself on Sacred Scripture, which presents homosexual acts as acts of grave depravity, tradition has always declared that 'homosexual acts are intrinsically disordered.' They are contrary to the natural law. They close the sexual act to the gift of life. They do not proceed from a genuine affective and sexual complementarity. Under no circumstances can they be approved".*
19. Item 2358. *"The number of men and women who have deep-seated homosexual tendencies is not negligible. This inclination, which is objectively disordered, constitutes for most of them a trial. They must be accepted with respect, compassion, and sensitivity. Every sign of unjust discrimination in their regard should be avoided. These persons are called to fulfil God's will in their lives and, if they are Christians, to unite to the sacrifice of the Lord's Cross the difficulties they may encounter from their condition".* The Catholic Church, while acknowledging that people can be born gay, says that homosexuality is *"objectively disordered"*.
20. Item 2359. *"Homosexual persons are called to chastity. By the virtues of self-mastery that teach them inner freedom, at times by the support of disinterested friendship, by prayer and sacramental grace, <u>they can and should gradually and resolutely approach Christian perfection</u>".* They just don't understand that Christ's death has made all who believe in Him 'perfect'.

Wow! It must be hard work being a Roman Catholic!

ABOUT THE AUTHOR

Paul Svensen, an Australian with Norwegian parents, grew up in Sydney's North Shore.

It was soon after building his first house that Paul, realising there was something missing from his life, found Jesus in a little stone Anglican church near his home.

Paul now lives in his adopted city of Canberra with his husband, Chan, and their Mini-Schnauzzer, Schnauzzie (of course). Chan and Paul are keen travellers and have been blessed to visit many countries, making lots of friends along the way.

www.ingramcontent.com/pod-product-compliance
Lightning Source LLC
Chambersburg PA
CBHW071216160426
43196CB00012B/2324